Merry Christmas
2005

Buckley

THE LEADERSHIP
OF JESUS
AND ITS LEGACY TODAY

J O H N   A D A I R

THE
PILGRIM
PRESS
Cleveland

Published in the USA and Canada by
The Pilgrim Press
700 Prospect Avenue East
Cleveland, Ohio 44115-1100
pilgrimpress.com

First published in 2001 by
The Canterbury Press Norwich
St Mary's Works, St Mary's Plain
Norwich, Norfolk NR3 3BH

Bible quotations are taken from The Revised Standard Version of the Bible
©1952 and 1971

© 2001 John Adair

John Adair has asserted his right under the Copyright, Design and Patents Act,
1988, to be identified as the Author of this Work.

The Pilgrim Press edition published 2002. All rights reserved.

06 05 04 03 02   5 4 3 2 1

Library of Congress Cataloging-in-Publication Data

Adair, John Eric, 1934-
    The leadership of Jesus and it's legacy today / John Adair.
        p. cm.
    ISBN 0-8298-1510-4 (pbk)
    1. Jesus Christ—Leadership. 2. Leadership—Religious aspects—
Christianity. I. Title.

BV4597.53.L43 A33 2002
232.9'04—dc21

                                                        2002035463

Contents

PART THREE:
THE LEGACY OF JESUS' LEADERSHIP

Introduction

Few individuals in history have been talked and written about as much as Jesus of Galilee. Yet, curiously, there have been few attempts to investigate the leadership of Jesus in the context of his times. My aim in this book has been to focus primarily on his natural qualities and abilities in order to reach a clear view of Jesus as a leader and to draw out any lessons for leadership that his life and teaching hold for our own times. My hope is that the book will both serve as an introduction and also stimulate others to explore further this neglected aspect of Jesus – his genius for leadership.

'Three things are too wonderful for me; four I do not understand,' wrote the author of the Book of Proverbs (30:18–19). 'The way of an eagle in the sky, the way of a serpent on a rock, the way of a ship on the high seas, and the way of a man with a maiden.' He could well have added 'the way of a leader with people'. For leadership, like love, is ultimately a mystery which no one fully understands. In its strongest forms it has always seemed to observers like a gift from heaven or a kind of magic. As Admiral Lord St Vincent, writing to Nelson – one of the comparatively few persons in history with a genius for leadership – declared: 'I never saw a man in our profession . . . who possessed the magic art of infusing the same spirit into others which inspired their own actions . . . all agree there is but one Nelson.'

Why does one person become accepted as a leader in a group rather than anyone else? What makes a leader inspirational? Why do some leaders transcend time and place, and attract followers who never knew them personally? These are some of the core questions in the study of leadership. They are not easy to answer, especially – as in the case of Jesus – where we lack most of the kinds of information that we should like to have had. But there is now a body of knowledge about leadership in general which will help us to interpret the relevant fragments that we do have, and then to assemble them like pieces of a jigsaw puzzle into a meaningful picture. Now is the time to try to see Jesus the leader – then and now.

A word about the plan of the book. In Part One I have asked myself three questions: What knowledge about leadership was present in the world before Jesus was born? Who were the leaders in the past who may have served as models for him? What kind of individuals in positions of leadership did he see in the society of his own time and place? A whole book could be written on each of these subjects, and therefore my four chapters are no more than outline sketches.

Part Two begins at Chapter Five with my attempt to reconstruct, again in outline, the story of the actual journey of Jesus as a leader. For a leader in the most literal sense is one who makes a physical journey with followers or companions. At this point I invite you to set aside hindsight, which is rather like asking you to go to see *Hamlet* as if you did not know what happens to the Prince of Denmark at the play's end. Can you imagine what it would be like for Jesus to be leading the way *without knowing what is to come next?* It is very difficult to do so because the four Gospels, our principal sources for the life of Jesus, are not written like that: they are impregnated with hindsight. 'History is lived forwards but it is written in retrospect,' wrote C. V. Wedgewood in her biography *William the Silent.* 'We know the end before we consider the beginning and we can never wholly recapture what it was to know the beginning only.' True, but it is worth trying to do so if you want to understand the full measure of Jesus' achievement as a leader.

What Jesus and his companions had in common on their journey was a vision – the 'kingdom of God' – and that vision is the subject of Chapter Six. Next, I turn to that first core question in leadership studies: why did some others – including leaders – involved in the common enterprise focused upon the 'kingdom of God' turn to Jesus and accept him as their leader? One reason is that Jesus not only clothed the vision with the imagery of his parables, but also – in a modern phrase – he 'lived the vision' and thereby made it seem both real and accessible. What were the qualities of leadership – the qualities required in that vision of the reality of the 'kingdom of God' – that people saw already present in him and others who belonged to the new and imminent order? Last but not least, Jesus gave some explicit teaching on leadership to back up his own example – what was his message? How far did his implicit teaching by example illustrate it?

Jesus of Galilee was a Jew who lived early in the first century, and it is impossible to understand him except in the context of his place and time, together with the world-view of his day. That is one side of the coin, but there is another. Jesus also transcends that context. For it is a fact that Jesus is one of the few individuals who seem somehow to rise above history, nationality, race, gender and creed – he is universal, he belongs to us all. Part Three seeks to place the leadership of Jesus in that universal context. What is his contribution to that timeless yet timely leadership that the world needs today? 'What genius does must be the best of all rules,' wrote Clausewitz, 'and theory cannot do better than to show how and why it is so.'

Perhaps this Introduction sounds just a bit academic. That is not my intention. To lead others you as a leader need to be able to inspire them, but where do you find inspiration yourself? Where are its wells in your own life? My deepest desire has been to step back out of the picture and let you come close to this extraordinary person. I imagine you sitting with Jesus, as if by the well of Jacob where that Samaritan woman came across him and found herself engaged in conversation which took her on a journey. You may offer him a drink from the well of your own hopes and intentions; what you may receive in return is living water that will refresh and inspire your spirit long after you have closed this book.

Part One

Leadership in Jesus' World

I

The Greek Teachers of Leadership

'Those having torches will pass them on to others.'

Plato

As Jesus stood on a hill near Gennesaret looking out over the Sea of Galilee he could have seen the evening sun falling on the white walls of Hippos, one of the Greek cities of the Decapolis – the Ten Cities – high on the south-western end of the blue mountainous plateau opposite. Eight miles into the hinterland lay the city of Gadara, the intellectual heart of the Decapolis. Menippos the Cynic satirist, Philodemus the Epicurean philosopher – a teacher of Virgil in Rome – and Meleager, a poet and anthologist who was born in the city, had all added to its reputation as a centre of Hellenic learning.

'If I am Syrian, what wonder?' Meleager had asked. 'Stranger, we dwell in one country, the world; one chaos gave birth to us all.' In the academic schools of Gadara – not restricted to Greeks by birth – young men of the region would acquire that cosmopolitan frame of mind, thinking of themselves as 'citizens of the world' and heirs to all the benefits of Greek civilization, its learning and spirit of inquiry. Within the Greek tradition they would encounter one strand that had explored the nature and practice of leadership. What kind of leader would flourish in a democratic society such as a Greek *polis*? The origin of this inquiry is to be found in Athens in the fifth century and particularly in its most influential philosopher, Socrates, whom his companions and fellow citizens sometimes called 'The Thinker'.

The Thinker – Socrates

Probably the son of a stonemason, a trade he may have practised himself for a period, Socrates was born around 470 BC. He served in the Athenian army in the war against Sparta as a 'hoplite' – one of the heavy-armoured spearmen who had to supply their own arms and armour and who fought in the phalanx. Socrates was renowned for both his courage in battle and also his remarkable endurance: in one winter campaign, for example, he continued to wear his threadbare clothes and to go barefoot as was his custom.

When he was about thirty-five years old, Socrates began to be a well-known figure in Athens, as he went about the streets or lingered in the marketplace engaged in discussion. Snub-nosed, with wide nostrils, protruding eyes and thick lips like a satyr, Socrates cut a strange figure in his simple garment with his bare feet and distinctive rolling or limping gait. But it was the extraordinary quality of his mind and the range of his interests that attracted a group of young men to his side as disciples. Among these disciples Plato and Xenophon are by far the best-known names.

Socrates wrote no books. Our main source of information about him are Plato's *Dialogues*, Xenophon's *Memoirs of Socrates* (known traditionally as the *Memorabilia*) and Aristophanes' satirical picture in *The Clouds*. It is uncertain how far Plato and Xenophon attributed their own opinions to their common master, and so it is difficult to discern the real Socrates. But there is one theory about leadership which we can be fairly sure does go back to Socrates because both Plato and Xenophon give us their versions of it. This theory can be neatly summed up in a modern proverbial saying: *Authority flows to the one who knows*. Here is Plato's version of the example of a ship's captain in *The Republic*:

> The sailors are quarrelling over the control of the helm. . . . They do not understand that the genuine navigator can only make himself fit to command a ship by studying the seasons of the year, sky, stars, and winds, and all that belongs to his craft; and they have no idea that, along with the science of

navigation, it is possible for him to gain, by instruction or practice, the skill to keep control of the helm whether some of them like it or not.

A much fuller exposition is to be found in the writings of Xenophon, the son of Gryllus, who lived from *c.* 428/7 to *c.* 354 BC. Xenophon came from a noble family in Athens and he could afford to serve in the cavalry. In his early twenties he sought election as one of the cavalry commanders. The generals or *strategoi* – the Greek word means literally 'the leaders of the army' – and other military commanders were all *elected* in Athens, and such an appointment was an important early rung on the ladder to political eminence for any ambitious young Athenian. What attracted Xenophon and his companions to Socrates was a sense that he alone had the key as to how to make themselves electable. In Xenophon's version below of the core theory, given here in the literary form of Socratic dialogue, Xenophon himself may well have been the original of the young Athenian cavalry commander in question.

The Case of the Young Cavalry Commander

One day Socrates, Xenophon narrates, met a newly elected young cavalry commander. Socrates asked him first why he had sought that office. The young man agreed under questioning by Socrates that it could not have been because he wanted to be first in the cavalry charge, for the mounted archers usually rode ahead of the commander into battle, nor could it have been simply in order to get himself known to everyone – for even madmen achieve that. He accepted Socrates' suggestion that it must be to leave the Athenian cavalry in better condition than when he found it. Xenophon, both a renowned authority on horsemanship and the author of a textbook on commanding cavalry, had no difficulty explaining in the dialogue what needs to be done to achieve that end. The young commander, for example, must improve the quality of the cavalry mounts; he must school new recruits – both horses and men – in equestrian skills and then teach the troopers their cavalry tactics.

'And have you considered how to make the men obey you?' continued Socrates. 'Because without that horses and men, however good and gallant, are of no use.'

'True, but what is the best way of encouraging them to obey, Socrates?' asked the young man.

'Well, I suppose you know that under all conditions human beings are most willing to obey those whom they believe to be the best. Thus in sickness they most readily obey the doctor, on board ship the pilot, on a farm the farmer, whom they think to be most skilled in their business.'

'Yes, certainly,' said his student.

'Then it is likely that in horsemanship too, one who clearly knows best what ought to be done will most easily gain the obedience of others.'

The key to leadership, then, is *knowledge*, or so Socrates thought. People will obey willingly only those whom they perceive to be better qualified or more knowledgeable than they are themselves in a particular situation. Therefore professional or technical excellence is a necessary prerequisite for holding a position of leadership responsibility. 'You must have noticed,' said Socrates to another man, 'that if he is incompetent, no one attempts to exercise authority over our harpists, choristers and dancers, nor over wrestlers? All who have authority over them can tell you where they learned their business.'

The tendency of people to follow a leader who knows what to do is strengthened in a time of crisis. In a discussion with Pericles, son of the famous statesman, which took place when an army from the Greek state of Boeotia was threatening Athens, Socrates made the additional point that such a crisis should be more to an effective leader's liking than a period of ease and prosperity, for it is easier to make things happen. He illustrated this point with the analogy Plato had also used, the behaviour of sailors at sea:

For confidence breeds carelessness, slackness, disobedience: for fear makes men more attentive, more obedient, more amenable to discipline. The behaviour of sailors is a case in point. So long as they have nothing to fear, they are, I believe, an unruly lot, but when they expect a storm or an attack, they not only carry out all orders, but watch in silence for the word of command like choristers.

There are arguably three main forms of authority in human affairs: the authority of *position* or rank, the authority of *personality*, and the authority of *knowledge*. Socrates clearly emphasized the latter. He pointed out that where women knew more than men – he instanced the weaving industry in Athens – they will be accepted as leaders.

The General – Xenophon

Xenophon was best known in the ancient world as a philosopher but he was also a man of action. Apparently against the advice of Socrates, Xenophon enlisted in the first large Greek mercenary army in history which the Persian prince Cyrus the Younger hired in a bid to replace his brother Artaxerxes II on the throne of Persia.

In his famous account of this Persian expedition, which immortalized the deeds of the Ten Thousand as they were known, Xenophon gives us vivid pen portraits of two contrasting styles of leadership displayed by two of the six Greek generals of the Ten Thousand. Both, in his view, fell short of the ideal.

Proxenus the Boeotian

Boeotia was a Greek city-state near Athens. Proxenus and Xenophon were friends, and it was through Proxenus, now a general, that Xenophon had been invited to join the expedition in Persia, in order to serve as one of the cavalry commanders.

Proxenus had spent much money on his education, especially for his lessons with a famous sophist called Gorgias of Leontoni, who was principally known as a teacher of rhetoric, but also later renowned as a literary stylist. Sophists – from the Greek word for a wise man – were a class of Greek teachers of rhetoric, philosophy and the art of successful living, noted for their clever, subtle, often specious reasoning. Ambitious for fame and wealth, Proxenus saw his office as a *strategos* or general as the first step on the road to attaining these ends in a fair and honourable way. As he was now about thirty years old he had no time to waste. Xenophon writes of him:

> He was a good commander for people of a gentlemanly type, but he was not capable of impressing his soldiers with a feeling of respect or fear for him. Indeed, he showed more diffidence in front of his soldiers than his subordinates showed in front of him, and it was obvious that he was more afraid of being unpopular with his troops than his troops were afraid of disobeying his orders. He imagined that to be a good general, and to gain the name for being one, it was enough to give praise to those who did well and to withhold it from those who did badly. The result was that decent people in his entourage liked him, but unprincipled people undermined his position, since they thought he was easily managed.

In other words, Proxenus liked to be liked. Now no one in their right mind enjoys being disliked, but popularity as an end in itself is not what a true leader seeks. Through his fear of becoming unpopular, Proxenus forfeited the respect of his soldiers – they lost their fear of disobeying his orders.

It could be argued that soldiers are a special case, in that, like Xenophon's beloved horses, they respond to a firm hand: you have to show them who is master, otherwise they do not respect or even fear you. Proxenus' style of leadership, we are told, worked better with educated fellow officers, who were more responsive to praise or lack of it and, being well-principled, appreciated his essential goodness. But soldiers – is it not true of us all? – are quick to sense a lack of confidence such as Proxenus' diffidence before them signalled. If Gorgias had taught him the art of communication he failed to practise it. And whatever teachings about command and tactics Proxenus may have acquired in such academic seminars, they gave him no confidence as a soldier. For, in truth, he had not learned the trade the hard way. Nor had the art of leadership in his case been forged in the fire of more junior responsibilities, under the hammer blows of experience.

Clearchus the Spartan

Clearchus was about fifty at the time, and he was the senior general. Clearchus had spent no money on acquiring an academic education. No Gorgias of Leontoni had taught him to write Greek like a stylist or to speak with an orator's graceful tricks and turns – it was not the Spartan way. Indeed the Spartans were renowned for their terseness of speech – our word *laconic* comes from the Greek word for a Spartan. Since childhood Clearchus – like all Spartan youths – had been inured to war. At the age of seven he would have moved into barracks, had his hair cut short and begun the Spartan military training based on discipline and exercise. At first the boys went barefoot and naked, and food was simple and scarce. This was to teach them to endure food shortages and also to steal so that later they could forage successfully. If caught stealing, they were punished for being poor at foraging, not for stealing as such. At the age of twelve years, the discipline became much harsher, with constant drill and exercise. One tunic had to serve each youth in winter and summer alike.

Among the Spartans courage was the highest virtue, and cowardice the worst crime. Fighting spirit was praised, but any overt display of anger or loss of temper was frowned upon. At twenty years of age Clearchus would have received the distinctive red cloak of a Spartan soldier, so famous that the Romans would adopt it – and one Roman soldier would drape his around the shoulders of Jesus before his crucifixion in an act of mockery. A stern disciplinarian, Clearchus had held various commands in the region of the Hellespont before Cyrus the Younger had commissioned him to raise the 10,400 Greek mercenaries to serve as the core of his Persian army.

This bid of Cyrus, the Persian paymaster of Clearchus, to replace his brother Artaxerxes II on the throne of Persia came to a disastrous end at the battle of Cunaxa (401 BC), not far from ancient Babylon, and Cyrus himself was killed. In the aftermath of the battle the victorious Persian commander offered to discuss surrender terms with the six Greek generals if they stayed where they were, but threatened to attack the Greeks if they moved from their camp. Clearchus took it upon himself to act as spokesman for his fellow generals to the Persian emissaries, but gave no indication to anyone what he was going to say. After sunset he summoned a meeting of the officers, briefly reviewed the options and then told them what they must do. They must break out of the cordon around their camp and head northwards that very night on the first stage of a long march to safety on the shores of the Black Sea, which lay some 800 miles away. As Xenophon records his famous account of the epic journey in *The Persian Expedition*, everyone sensed that only Clearchus could lead them out of mortal danger:

> On receiving their instructions the generals and captains went away and carried them out; and from then on Clearchus was in command, and they were his subordinates. This was not the result of an election, but because they realised that he was the one man who had the right sort of mind for a commander, while the rest of them were inexperienced.

This story seems to illustrate perfectly the Socratic doctrine that *Authority flows to the one who knows*. Alone Clearchus seemed to know what to do. He was clear and decisive about the way ahead when his fellow generals, younger and less experienced, probably felt as much at a loss as their men – and as anxious as well. In the hour of crisis, Clearchus inspired confidence. But not much else! As Xenophon, a keen observer of human nature, goes on to note:

> As for Clearchus' great qualities as a soldier, they appear in the facts that he was fond of adventure, ready to lead an attack on the enemy by day or night, and that, when he was in an awkward position, he kept his head, as everyone agrees who was with him anywhere. It was said that he had all the qualities of leadership which a man of his sort could have.

He had an outstanding ability for planning means by which an army could get supplies, and seeing that they appeared; and he was also well able to impress on those who were with him that Clearchus was a man to be obeyed. He achieved this result by his toughness. He had a forbidding appearance and a harsh voice. His punishments were severe ones and were sometimes inflicted in anger, so that there were times when he was sorry himself for what he had done. With him punishment was a matter of principle, for he thought that any army without discipline was good for nothing; indeed, it is reported that he said that a soldier ought to be more frightened of his own commander than of the enemy if he was going to turn out one who could keep a good guard, or abstain from doing harm to his own side, or go into battle without second thoughts.

So it happened that in difficult positions the soldiers would give him complete confidence and wished for no one better. On these occasions, they said that his forbidding look seemed positively cheerful, and his toughness appeared as confidence in the face of the enemy, so that it was no longer toughness to them but something to make them feel safe. On the other hand, when the danger was over and there was a chance of going away to take service under someone else, many of them deserted him, since he was invariably tough and savage, so that the relations between his soldiers and him were like those of boys and a schoolmaster.

Clearchus had all the military virtues, notably bravery. He was a good manager as well. Unlike Proxenus, he was respected and feared by the officers and soldiers alike. But they did not like him – indeed on one occasion a soldier threatened to strike him with a hatchet – and the best soldiers would choose to serve under other commanders if they had the choice. To Xenophon's mind, Clearchus lacked the key quality that any excellent leader should possess: the ability to inspire a willing and enthusiastic obedience in his soldiers. Such a leader, deeply respected by his men, might inspire a certain awe in them but not the servility of slaves or the resentful compliance of schoolboys under a domineering schoolmaster. The test would be whether or not they made this general their first choice when they had the freedom to re-enlist.

Xenophon, the Athenian

In *The Persian Expedition* Xenophon writes about himself in the third person, and so it is not too difficult to take him as our third case-study in leadership – it is how he saw himself. He was elected as one of the successors to Clearchus and the other five Greek generals whom the Persians invited to a feast ostensibly to discuss peace terms and then – during the meal – butchered in an act of treachery not long after Cunaxa. Having been taught leadership by Socrates, what kind of leadership would Xenophon display? Doubtless he thought hard about that question. Obviously he did not want to be another Clearchus, nor did he want to err too far in the opposite direction of courting popularity and appearing weak as Proxenus had done.

According to his own account Xenophon, then aged about twenty-six, gave energetic and inspiring leadership to the Ten Thousand as they struggled to the Black Sea skirmishing along the way. One example of his outstanding gift as a leader occurred in a skirmish against a hostile tribe called the Carduci. They had occupied some high ground overlooking the road ahead, and had to be removed. Xenophon spotted a summit that would command their position and led a mixed force of 500 skirmishers and hoplites up the steep slope towards it. The rest of the Ten Thousand in the valley, and indeed some of the Persian cavalry in close pursuit under their general Tissaphernes on the hills behind them, were like spectators standing or sitting in the stands at the games to what followed:

> Then there was a lot of shouting, from the Greek army cheering on its men on the one side and from Tissaphernes' people cheering on their men on the other side. Xenophon rode along the ranks on horseback, urging them on. 'Soldiers,' he said, 'consider that it is for Greece you are fighting now, that you

are fighting your way to your children and your wives, and that with a little hard work now, we shall go on the rest of our way unopposed.'

Soteridas, a man from Sicyon, said: 'We are not on a level, Xenophon. You are riding on horseback, while I am wearing myself out with a shield to carry.'

The story illustrates how the Greeks thought of themselves as equals, and the fact that their leaders depended upon their consent to be led. But it could be awkward when they asserted their sense of democracy and equality in a crisis like this one where there was no time for debate. As the commander on the spot, Xenophon had several options open to him. He could have ignored the man. Or he could have threatened him. Or he could conceivably have had him arrested and punished later. Xenophon took none of these courses. Writing of himself in the third person he tells us what happened next:

When Xenophon heard this, he jumped down from his horse, pushed Soteridas out of the ranks, took his shield away from him and went forward on foot as fast as he could, carrying the shield. He happened to be wearing a cavalry breastplate as well, so that it was heavy going for him. He kept on encouraging those in front to keep going and those behind to join up with them, though struggling along behind them himself. The other soldiers, however, struck Soteridas and threw stones at him and cursed him until they forced him to take back his shield and continue marching. Xenophon then remounted and, so long as the going was good, led the way on horseback. When it became impossible to ride, he left his horse behind and hurried ahead on foot. And so they got to the summit before the enemy.

Note that it was the other soldiers who shamed Soteridas into taking back his shield. Although Xenophon, burdened with a heavy cavalry breastplate, eventually fell back behind the ranks as the men rushed up the hill, yet he encouraged the men forward and urged them to keep their battle order. Eventually he

remounted and led his soldiers from the front, at first on horse
and then again on foot.

Once the Greeks had gained the summit the Carduci turned
and fled in all directions. The Persian cavalry under Tissaphernes, distant onlookers of the contest, also turned their
bridles and withdrew.

Then the vanguard of the Greek army were able to move
forward and descend through the mountain pass into a fertile
plain beside the Tigris. There they refreshed themselves before
facing the fearsome rigours of a winter march amid the snow-
covered Armenian highlands. Eventually, in the summer of the
following year, the army reached the safety of the Hellespont,
the narrow straits dividing Europe from Asia. They owed much
to Xenophon who, not long afterwards, became the com-
mander-in-chief of the Ten Thousand.

Xenophon spent part of his later career in active military
service mainly as an adviser to the two Spartan kings. At that
time Athens was in political turmoil. Socrates had been executed
and Xenophon himself banished – so it was natural for him to
find refuge among the Spartans whose virtues and customs he
admired. The rest of his time he spent as a prolific writer on a
whole range of subjects, historical, political and practical.
Among his books his *Memoirs of Socrates* and *The Education of Cyrus* can be described as the world's first books on
leadership.

In the latter, known in antiquity by its Greek title *Cyropaedia*,
a philosophical dialogue about the education of Cyrus the Great,
who in fact does little more than lend his name to the ideal ruler
at work to create the ideal state, Xenophon advocates that such
a ruler 'should demonstrate that in summer he can endure the
heat, and in winter the cold; and he should show that in difficult
times he can endure the hardships as well as, if not better than,
his men'. Moreover, a leader should rejoice with them if any
good befell them, and sympathize with them if any ills overtook
them, showing himself eager to help in times of stress. 'It is in
these respects that you should somehow go hand-in-hand with
them,' wrote Xenophon. 'All this contributes to the leader being
loved by his men.' Xenophon added the interesting observation

that it was actually easier for the leader to endure heat and cold, hunger and thirst, want and hardship, than his followers. 'The general's position, and the very consciousness that nothing he does escapes notice, lightens the burden for him.' Julius Caesar studied the *Cyropaedia* carefully, and his own inspiring conduct as a general is a commentary upon it.

What really interests Xenophon is the way a true leader inspires those around him. It is something more than having superior professional or technical knowledge, something to do with the human spirit. Mere compliance to orders gives way to a willing and wholehearted enthusiasm for the work in hand. Xenophon had often sailed in Athenian triremes, powered by oarsmen drawn from the poorest classes, and so he could write from experience:

> On a man-of-war, when the ship is on the high seas and the rowers must toil all day to reach port, some rowing-masters can say and do the right thing to sharpen the men's spirits and make them work with a will. Other rowing-masters are so unintelligent that it takes them more than twice the time to finish the same voyage. Here they land bathed in sweat, with mutual congratulations, rowing-master and seamen. There they arrive with dry skin; they hate their master and he hates them.

What is it that will 'sharpen the men's spirit and make them work with a will'? Xenophon's mind ranged back to the generals he had known, who also differed widely from one another in this respect.

> For some make their men unwilling to work and to take risks, disinclined and unwilling to obey, except under compulsion, and actually proud of defying their commander: yes, and they cause them to have no sense of dishonour when something disgraceful occurs. Contrast the genius, the brave and skilful leader: let him take over the command of these same troops, or of others if you like. What effect has he on them? They are ashamed to do a disgraceful act, think it better to obey,

and take a pride in obedience, working cheerfully, every man and all together, when it is necessary to work. Just as a love of work may spring up in the mind of a private soldier here and there, so a whole army under the influence of a good leader is inspired by love of work and ambition to distinguish itself under the commander's eye. Let this be the feeling of the rank and file for their commander, then he is the best leader – it is not a matter of being best with bow and javelin, nor riding the best horse and being foremost in danger, nor being the perfect mounted warrior, but of being able to make his soldiers feel that they must follow him through fire and in any adventure. So, too, in private industries, the man in authority – bailiff or manager – who can make the workers keen, industrious, and persevering – he is the man who gives a lift to the business and swells the profits.

Xenophon concluded his book on estate management by declaring that he had no envy for the master with the fullest power to punish the bad and reward the strenuous workmen, whose appearance in the fields is a matter of indifference to the men at work. He would say as much about a general. 'But, if *at the sight of him* they bestir themselves, and a spirit of determination and rivalry and eagerness to excel falls on every workman, then I should say "This man has a touch of the kindly native about him." And this, in my judgement, is *the greatest thing in every operation that makes any demand on the labour of men.'*

Such leadership cannot be learnt, Xenophon believed, by someone who just sees it or is told about it once. 'My position is rather that anyone who is to have this ability requires training and must also be naturally talented and above all favoured by the gods. For I'm not quite convinced that this power to win willing obedience is entirely human rather than divine: it is clearly granted to those who are truly committed to self education.'

'Leader of the Greeks' – Alexander the Great

The written word can inspire. Alexander, son of King Philip II of Macedon, was given Xenophon's *The Persian Expedition* to read, probably by his tutor Aristotle. The account of the great march of the Ten Thousand through the Persian empire certainly helped to inflame his ardour to lead a Greek army into Persia. When Alexander's father died and he inherited his formidable Macedonian army, he set about realizing his vision of conquering that vast empire that sprawled across the known East. Alexander certainly possessed that 'magic art of infusing the same spirit into others, which inspired their own actions' of which Xenophon had already written and which Nelson would one day exemplify. He shared fully in the dangers, hardships and toils of his men. It is as if he was *among* his men, not *over* them. He led from the front. Here is an example of Alexander in action as a great leader.

Imagine a desolate desert of barren rocks and sand and scrub, scorched by the sun. It is midsummer, hence the furnace-like heat. Across this arid plain in Asia Minor, called the Gedrosian desert, marches Alexander's Greek army of some 30,000 foot soldiers with cavalry units in the rear. The best and most reliable historian of his conquests, Arrian – a Greek writer of the second century AD with the Latin name Flavius Arrianus – tells the story of what happened next:

> Alexander, like everyone else, was tormented by thirst, but he was none the less marching on foot at the head of his men. It was all he could do to keep going, but he did so, and the result (as always) was that the men were better able to endure their misery when they saw it was equally shared. As they toiled on, a party of light infantry, which had gone off looking for water, found some, just a wretched little trickle collected in a shallow gully. They scooped up with difficulty what they could and hurried back, with their priceless treasure, to Alexander; then, just before they reached him, they tipped the water into a helmet and gave it to him. Alexander, with a word of thanks for the gift, took the helmet and, in full

view of his troops, poured the water on the ground. So extraordinary was the effect of this action that the water wasted was as good as a drink for every man in the army. I cannot praise this act too highly; it was a proof, if anything was, not only of his power of endurance, but also of his genius for leadership.

Physical height was deeply associated with superiority in the ancient mind, possibly because tall men had an advantage in hand-to-hand fighting and tended to be chosen as war-leaders. The prophet Samuel, for example, seems to have chosen Saul as king partly because he was a head taller than the other Israelites. Herod the Great was a tall man too. But Alexander was less than middle height. When he first sat on the throne of Cyrus the Great his servants had to replace the footstool with a table. When he met some Persian emissaries they initially made their obeisances to one of his staff who was the tallest man in the royal party. (The Medes, incidentally, first introduced high-heeled shoes for men to give their leaders extra height; Augustus Caesar, too, wore shoes with built-up heels, a practice not unknown among modern political leaders who lack stature.) But Alexander did have physical features which suggested to others his genius for leadership. His portraits emphasized his large, staring, luminous eyes. He could evidently speak effectively and move men's emotions with his words. His enthusiasm and energy seemed to be boundless. Add to these assets his royal birth and unbroken string of successes, and it is not difficult to see why an aura of the extraordinary or even superhuman developed around the young man. But at the core of it lay his extraordinary gifts as a leader.

As a general, Alexander possessed that all-important power of being able to sum up the inevitably confused situations on battlefields and then take the appropriate action in a calm, effective way. He had a sure intuition – a feeling for the real situation long before it becomes plain to others. But it is as an inspirer or motivator of soldiers that Alexander really excelled. He shared fully in the men's dangers, as the scars of his wounds testified. Alexander would remind them on occasion that he ate the same food as they did. He was highly visible. In the siege preparations against Tyre, for example, when a massive stone pier had to be constructed in the harbour under enemy fire, Alexander was always on the spot. Sometimes he worked alongside the men. He gave clear instructions, but he was also a great encourager of others, backing up his words with rewards for outstanding effort. In the assault on Tyre which followed, he fought hard himself but was ever on the watch for any acts of conspicuous courage in the face of danger among his men. After a siege or battle he was especially good at naming those who had distinguished themselves in front of their companions – all Greeks loved personal fame.

Of course Alexander could not have known as individuals the Macedonian contingent, let alone all the Greeks in his army. But it was part of his genius as a leader that they felt he did. He certainly took care to meet their individual needs. Arrian recorded plenty of examples of Alexander's humanity and care for his soldiers as individuals and persons. He never regarded them as mere wielders of spears or swords, but rather as his companions and brothers-in-arms, and they responded accordingly. After one battle, Arrian writes, 'for the wounded he showed deep concern; he visited them all and examined their wounds, asking each man how and in what circumstances his wound was received, and allowing him to tell his story and exaggerate as much as he pleased'.

It was this care for individual needs, this deep sense of comradeship and humanity, that endeared Alexander to his troops. It appears again in his thoughtful concern for the young Macedonian hoplites who had hastily married on the eve of the expedition, perhaps on the grounds that they might not return from the wars. Feeling that some consideration was due to these men, Alexander dismissed them at the end of the first summer, sending them home to spend the winter with their wives. 'No act of Alexander's ever made him better beloved by his native troops,' commented Arrian.

The Greeks were individualists and they responded to a leader who related to them as individuals. Alexander understood that fact well. He understood that his commanders and soldiers would excel themselves if they knew his eye rested upon them and that their deeds and names were recorded in his mind. Of course he could not know the names of all the 30,000 or more Greek soldiers, but he did know the names of his officers. Xenophon, whom Alexander had read on the subject, laid considerable stress on this importance of a leader learning the names of his people. It is a point that is as relevant today as it was in classical times, for human nature does not change. In the *Cyropaedia*, Xenophon writes:

> Now Cyrus made a study of this; for he thought it passing strange that, while every mechanic knows the names of the tools of his trade and the physician knows the names of all the instruments he uses, the general should be so foolish as not to know the names of the officers under him.

Xenophon pointed out that those men who are conscious of being personally known to their general do more good and abstain more from evil than any others. Cicero, incidentally, who also read this passage in Xenophon, applied much the same principle to politics. He stocked his exceptional memory with the names of some thousands of the leading citizens of Rome. This knowledge, he found, greatly helped him when it came to gaining election and holding office in Rome. In a later age, Napoleon claimed to know the names of every officer in the *Grand Armée*.

Above all, Alexander possessed a great dream or vision of his destiny and the destiny of Greece as the civilizing agent in the world. As 'Leader of the Greeks', he gave his compatriots a sense of purpose and that helped to give them unity. He inspired his officers and men with this energetic vision. Ovid's words could well apply to Alexander: 'He was a leader of leaders.'

The source of the troubles that almost broke this matchless army lay in its very success. How often success leads to failure! As victory succeeded victory and the epic unfolded, a group of obsequious courtiers around the young king (Alexander was only twenty-two years old when he crossed the Hellespont) fed him with a heady mixture of proper compliments and insincere flattery. They blew up the bladder of his conceit, ascribing the string of successes and conquests to Alexander's own courage and brilliance as a general, and not to the true cause: the combination of the army's superb fighting qualities as a battle-winning team and Alexander's leadership. It is a fatal error for any strategic leader – the head of a whole organization – to exaggerate their own importance at the expense of the self-esteem of others.

This inflated self-importance or pride was challenged one night with dramatic and tragic consequences. Some six years had passed since the expedition had set out from Greece, and the army was encamped at Samarkand. Alexander and some of his officers had been drinking heavily. The flatterers were at work plying Alexander with the notion that he was superior to the very gods to whom he had been sacrificing that day, superior even to the god Heracles. Only envy deprived him of the divine honours due to him, these flatterers told him. This was too much for Cleitus, veteran commander of the Companion cavalry, who was as drunk as his master. In angry tones he denounced such insults to the gods. Moreover, he continued, they grossly exaggerated the marvellous nature of Alexander's achievements, none of which were mere personal triumphs of his own; on the contrary, most of them were the work of Macedonians as a whole. The young king lost his temper and in the ensuing brawl he speared his friend Cleitus to death.

Despite Alexander's subsequent remorse for the killing of Cleitus, he had not learnt his lesson. In the course of time he became in effect the ruler of the old Persian empire. Persian noblemen at his court now joined forces with the Greek flatterers in his entourage to stir up Alexander's pretensions to the status of a god. The Persian and Greek contexts were quite different regarding the cultural forms of leadership. The Persians were already worshipping Alexander. For the subjects of his new eastern domains deemed it inconceivable that a great conqueror such as Alexander was not a god in human form.

The Greeks were happy to concede to Alexander the descent he claimed from Heracles – on his coins he is depicted as wearing the ram's horns of the hero-god – and to acknowledge him as a more than ordinary person, a genius. Neither view committed them to the doctrine that Alexander was a living god before whom they must prostrate themselves on their faces in the traditional act of worship in the East. They saw Alexander as a leader who was their companion, albeit one better than them in all respects; in their relations with him they wanted to remain on the domain where reasoned argument and concession on both sides was possible, not to descent into oriental submission to a despot who claimed the divine prerogatives of a god. Being Greeks they knew how to wait for the right moment and then how to make their points as tactfully as possible to Alexander.

The day for speaking the truth to Alexander, at least about his zeal for the continuance of the long expedition of conquest, came eventually on the western bank of the river Hypasis in India. Beyond it lay green jungles and plains, already alive in Alexander's fertile imagination with Indian princes and princesses, with rubies, sapphires and pearls in abundance, lords of the largest herds of the most courageous elephants on the continent . . . But the monsoon rains, incessant for days, had dampened the men's appetite for more adventure. Some swore that they would march no further, not even if Alexander himself led them. When rumours of this discontent reached him, Alexander called a meeting of his officers. But his plan to cross the river was greeted with a long silence. At last Coenus, a brave Companion, spoke up and told Alexander the truth as tactfully as he could – that the army was now longing to return home. 'No longer in poverty and obscurity, but famous and enriched by the treasure you have enabled them to win. Do not try to lead men who are unwilling to follow you; if their heart is not in it, you will never find the old spirit or courage. . . . Sir, if there is one thing above all others a successful man should know, it is when to stop. Assuredly for a commander like yourself, with an army like ours, there is nothing to fear from any army; but luck, remember, is an unpredictable thing, and against what it may bring no man has any defence.'

A burse of spontaneous applause followed these plain words. With a flash of temper Alexander abruptly dismissed them. Next day he told his officers that, while not wishing to put pressure on anyone, he at least intended to continue the advance. For two days he awaited a change of heart. But officers and men remained silent; they were angry at Alexander's outburst and determined not to let him influence them. Using the excuse of the sacrificial omens, Alexander gave in. His message that the army would turn homewards caused much rejoicing. It is said to have been Alexander's only defeat.

Probably for political reasons, more than out of vanity, as they marched homewards Alexander began persistently to put pressure on his Greek officers to prostrate themselves before him. Maintaining law and order in a vast empire when the ruler is perforce absent is much easier, the Persians had discovered, if the ruler is perceived by his subjects to be a god. The worship of such a single man served to focus loyalty and to create unity amid the diverse tribes and nations that made up the patchwork of empire.

For the most part his Greek officers refused to comply: such an act was completely against their traditions. In the event, Alexander compromised. While accepting the obeisances of his Persian subjects – lying flat on their faces before him – he promised the Greeks that the need to prostrate themselves would not in future arise. To confirm that dispensation, Alexander organized a mass wedding in the Persian fashion for eighty of his Companions. He led the way, as always, by marrying two wives himself. 'Alexander was always capable of putting himself on a footing of equality and comradeship with his subordinates,' wrote Arrian, 'and everyone felt that this act of his was the best proof of his ability to do so.'

The Persians had introduced prostration as part of a novel method of creating an aura of divinity around their kings. Herodotus told the story of how it came about. A Mede called Deioces, who lived in the ancient time when the Medes had escaped from under the yoke of Assyria, made a local reputation as an arbiter of disputes by his fairness and integrity. Eventually the Medes chose him as their first king. Deioces ordered his subjects to build him a palace, which became the centre-piece of a new capital city, ringed on its commanding hill by seven high walls. As far as possible he then vanished from their sight, surrounding himself with a new ceremonial of royalty and strict protocol. For example, it was forbidden to laugh or spit in the royal presence. 'This solemn ceremonial was designed as a safeguard against his contemporaries, men as good as himself in birth and personal quality, with whom he had been brought up in early years,' wrote Herodotus. 'There was a risk that if they saw him habitually, it might lead to jealously and resentment, and plots would follow; but if nobody saw him, the legend would grow that he was a being of a different order from mere men.'

One can see how the Persian method of creating a divine aura by creating *distance* between the ruler and the people is in clear contrast to the Greek tradition of maintaining *closeness* between leader and followers. In the latter, leaders are prized who share the same hardships and dangers, and eat the same food. That principle applied even in such Greek states as Sparta which had kings. In the one culture, the head of state is virtually invisible; in the other, he is expected to be among his people. The drawback of the more democratic concept, of course, is that closeness dispels any notion of divinity. If a man is seen and known at close quarters it is unlikely that people will believe him to be divine. Therefore the Persian method was antithetical to leadership. It was designed to create despotic rulers, not leaders. The logical climax of creating this artificial *distance* was the declaration of the king's divinity.

A direct descendant of Deioces four generations later, Cyrus the Great, is said to have been the monarch who introduced prostration into Persia. Incidentally, he balanced the invocation of worship directed towards himself with a remarkable toleration to other religions in his domains, such as the cult of Marduk at Babylon. Cyrus even allowed the Jewish exiles to return from Babylon and rebuild their temple in Jerusalem. Hence, in part, his reputation for wisdom in the Greek world, and why young Greeks like Xenophon revered his memory.

The infusion of Persian commanders and soldiers into the army in ever-growing numbers did impose immense strains on its unity. Only the remarkable personality and presence of Alexander, his consistent leadership, could hold this flock of Greek rams and Persian he-goats together. After Alexander's death the unity of his army disintegrated, for it had all depended too much on him. Alexander's generals who succeeded him were lost without him. Some years later, when they met to try to find that lost unity and peace, they chose to come together before his empty throne in his old tent. In death, as in life, Alexander was the only one who could hold them together.

Perhaps as they stood again in that familiar tent, Alexander's former generals – now his quarrelling successors – recalled their last sight of their young master as he lay on his deathbed under the tent's shade. The army had reached Babylon on its meandering way home, not two miles from the battlefield of Cunaxa where Xenophon had first encountered the Persian hosts. As word had spread among the Greeks in the now polyglot army that Alexander lay dying, the veterans crowded into the centre to see him, their hearts full of grief. They were bewildered, too, at the thought of what lay in store for them without Alexander as their leader. At last, on that sad Tuesday, beside the waters of Babylon, they were allowed into the royal tent, filing past Alexander on his couch in their thousands. Lying speechless as the men passed, Alexander could be seen struggling to raise his head. In his eyes, once so famous for their intensity, there seemed to be a look of recognition for each individual as he passed. He was then thirty-two years and eight months old.

The Greeks were too intelligent to recognize Alexander's genius for leadership as anything more than a divine gift, despite his attempts to have himself numbered among the gods. The Persian doctrine, that a great empire could only be ruled by a king who was worshipped as a god, was destined to prevail, however, at first among Alexander's successors in Syria and Egypt, and then among the Romans when they moved from being a republic to being an empire. Many European kings, presidents and dictators in modern times have applied the same Persian or Eastern formula of creating a godlike aura by splendid courts and remoteness from their people, with varying degrees of success.

The death of Alexander in 323 BC precipitated a series of civil wars among his generals, who were known collectively as the Successors. Control of Judaea, the land of the Jews, was disputed between dynasties that traced descent from two Successors: the Seleucids who ruled over Syria and much of Asia, and the Ptolemies in Egypt. The conquests of Alexander and their aftermath in these shifting, warring states had spread the Greek language and Hellenistic culture throughout the East. New Greek cities like those of Decapolis sprang up, while older cities like Damascus and Jerusalem were rebuilt or refurbished with public buildings in the Greek style. The Greek concept of leadership, exemplified in the life and writings of Xenophon, was part of this cultural inheritance, but how far it influenced those in positions of authority in the Gentile world must be a matter of conjecture.

In Judaea this Hellenistic culture ground like a tectonic plate against another ancient and underlying one – the deep Semitic tradition – that was antithetical to it. In the context of these Hellenic civil wars in the East, the Jews showed that they were willing to fight for their political independence in order to preserve their own unique Semitic culture and way of life. What ideas of leadership did they imbibe from their past? Who were the great models of leadership that they found in their own sacred scriptures?

2

Great Leaders of the Bible

When leaders are worthy of respect, the people are willing to work for them. When their virtue is worthy of admiration, their authority can be established.

Haunanzi (Chinese philosopher, 4th century BC)

A legendary Assyrian general named Holophernes is riding down the coast of Canaan at the head of a vast army of 130,000 men, on an expedition to punish the western vassals of his emperor Nebuchadnezzar for refusing contributions to his wars in the east. All have submitted and paid up except the inhabitants of the ridge of hills which rise east of the coastal plain. 'What nation is this that lives in the hill-country?' Holophernes demands of his Canaanite allies. 'How big is their army? What gives them their power and strength? Why are they the only people of the west who have refused to come and meet me?'

The answer, given by their spokesman in this story from the apocryphal Book of Judith, is a summary in three terse paragraphs of the history of Israel. The hill-dwellers, explains an ally, are descendants of the Chaldeans, from the mouth of the Euphrates. Their ancestors travelled up-river from there to northern Mesopotamia, where they lived for many years, and then drifted south-west into the land of Canaan, where they grew rich in gold, silver and livestock.

Because of a famine, these nomads went down to Egypt and flourished there until the mushrooming of their numbers alarmed the Egyptians, who enslaved and persecuted them as a dangerous minority. In revenge, they appealed to their God to send plagues on the Egyptians, who turned them out to wander across Sinai and Edom (today's Negev) until they reached the country east of the Jordan. Crossing the river, they drove out the local inhabitants with their God's help, and have occupied ever since the ridges looking down to the Mediterranean. On the whole, he concludes, it is better not to meddle with them. When their God chooses to intervene on their behalf in their quarrels with other peoples, the result can be humiliating.

This summary leaves much out, but it emphasizes usefully two points central to the biblical story. The first thing their neighbours know about the Jews is that they come from elsewhere. The other is their geographical situation in the land they considered God had promised to them. In spite of the promise, they never really commanded the plains of Palestine, or tried to. They remained hill-dwellers, clinging to the heights which run north and south from the borders of Syria to Sinai, from their capital and sanctuary, Jerusalem, in the middle of the range. And their more distant origins lay in the immense deserts of Arabia and then in the land of Mesopotamia, the place of origin of their founding-father and first great leader – Abraham.

The Patriarch – Abraham

The Jews in the days of Jesus revered Abraham as their great ancestor, as they do to this day. Abraham holds a unique place in Jewish affections; he is their father, as they are each of them his children. As heirs to the promises made by God to Abraham righteous Jews saw death as a gathering to him; to die is to be received in 'Abraham's bosom' (Luke 16:22). The very name of Abraham is a pledge that the same mercy he received will be enjoyed by his 'posterity' (Luke 1:55). And, finally, to be with Abraham and his great sons, to 'sit at table with Abraham, Isaac, and Jacob in the kingdom of heaven' (Matthew 8:11) will be the destiny of the Israelite who faithfully keeps God's law.

Abraham – which means 'father of many nations' – is in fact a surname conferred by God on a man known as the son of Terah. He was a semi-nomad of the Aramaean people. One tradition says he was born in Ur in northern Mesopotamia, a city of the Chaldeans who were Aramaeans by origin. Both Aramaeans and Chaldeans were Semite peoples – so named in the eighteenth century after Shem, one of Noah's sons. The

Semites can only be identified by similarities in their languages. They appear to be offshoots of pure desert nomad tribes by origin, the descendants of those who moved out of the deserts of what is now Saudi Arabia in migrational waves. Over a millennium or more they eventually settled in, among other areas, the northern fertile crescent of rain-fed land that arcs like a bow from the Mediterranean to eastern Mesopotamia. The migration of Abraham and his clan around 2300 BC into the land of Canaan can be best understood in this context.

The Jews are not the only great Semite nation to trace its descent from Abraham. Ishmael, the son of Abraham by Hagar – his wife's Egyptian handmaiden – is regarded by the Arabs as their founder. Driven out into the desert with his mother because of Sarah's jealousy, Ishmael grew up to be a famous archer in the wilderness of Paran, the central part of what we now call Sinai. The prophet Muhammad claimed a direct descent from him. The Muslim feast of *Eid-at-Kabir* – the Great Feast – celebrates God's divine intervention to prevent Abraham from sacrificing his other son Isaac, thus outlawing human sacrifice.

By contrast, the Jews traced their own descent through Isaac, who married his cousin Rebekah when he was forty years old. Their twin sons, Esau and Jacob, were born some twenty years later. By deceit Jacob won for himself Esau's birthright and paternal blessing. His concluding days were passed at Goshen in Egypt, where one of his twelve sons, Joseph, held high office. Isaac and Jacob and their descendants believed themselves inheritors of the land of Canaan which God, it was claimed, had 'promised' to their great ancestor and father Abraham.

What kind of leader was Abraham? The Book of Deuteronomy records that the Jews, now settled in Canaan, were commanded to bring the first fruits of the soil as a thank-offering to God, prefaced by a declaration of faith which begins: 'A wandering Aramaean was my father; and he went down into Egypt and sojourned there, few in number; and there he became a nation, great, mighty, and populous (26:5).' Abraham was a chief of a 'wandering' or semi-nomadic tribe of Aramaeans with a past that reached back to the Arabian deserts. The role of the *shaykh* in camel-rearing Bedouin tribes of the Arabian deserts

– still the thoroughbreds of the Semitic peoples – give the best idea of what Abraham must have been like as a leader.

The Hebrew word for a leader in this sense is *nasi*. It possibly comes from a three-consonant verbal root which means 'to lift up', hence 'someone who is lifted up, exalted'. The same root appears in Arabic with the meaning 'to rise'.

The Hittite people living around Hebron, who were not themselves Semites by origin, used this word *nasi* of Abraham. In English, in the King James' Bible, it was translated as 'mighty prince'. The context was a meeting where they gave Abraham some land so that he could bury his wife Sarah. Although a prince or *princeps* in Latin was originally no more than a chief man or leading citizen, in course of time it came to mean a monarch or a king's son. In fact Abraham was no more than a tribal chief, not a prince in our sense.

Abraham's more customary title of *patriarch* also has overtones of leadership. It is Greek in origin, for an *archos* is a chief (from the verb *archein*, to be first, hence *arche*, beginning). In modern English, *archos* or *arch* is almost solely used as a prefix, as in *arch*-bishop, *arch*-deacon, *arch*-duke and *arch*-angel, though Shakespeare speaks of 'my worthy *arch* and patron' in *King Lear*. But in the biblical context a *patriarch* is the first or chief of a *patria*, a lineage or people. In the fifth century AD but in a rather different sense – more as 'chief father' – *patriarch* became the title for heads of clusters of Christian dioceses.

A patriarchal system of society or government, it follows, is rule by the senior male of the family or tribe. A Bedouin chief fits into that category in some respects, but not others. Until recent times, he – always a he – was chosen from among the suitable candidates in a restricted number of tribal families. The Arabic *shaykh*, related to the verb 'to be old' or 'to grow older', means an old man, elder or chief. In Hebrew, the word for 'elder' literally means beard. So the notions of age – being a tribal 'elder' (in those days anyone over thirty years) – and being a tribal leader are closely linked. The *shaykh* was often chosen for his leadership qualities, such as courage in battle, generosity or the willingness to put others' needs before his own, and a lack of arrogance.

In the patriarchal society of the ancient world fathers did have absolute power over of the lives of their children. They could even put them to death as a punishment or make a human sacrifice of them – Abraham came close to offering Isaac to God. But the conditions of life in the desert bred among the nomadic Semites their own form of democracy – a natural democracy which bears comparison with the civic forms that evolved out of similar forms of early tribal society in cities like Athens and Rome.

In desert nomadic tribes the chief or leader is not an absolute ruler: he cannot order his fellow tribesmen to comply with his wishes or tyrannize them. The chief's prime functions were leadership in war or on intertribal raids, and being the arbitrator in disputes. In making his judgments the tribal chief worked in harmony with a group of elders, men of influence or means, or men who together formed the repository of oral tradition concerning tribal laws and customs. His *majlis* or council, often held in the open air, was the place where, after much talk, matters were resolved. All members of the tribe had the right to attend the *majlis* and make their personal requests to the *shaykh*. Consequently the Persian tradition of creating kings and making access to them through 'proper channels' of inter-mediaries is totally alien to the desert tribes.

In her account of her travels in *Bedouin Tribes of the Euphrates*, the Victorian writer Lady Anne Blunt described the Bedouin tribe as 'the purest form of democracy to be found in the world'. A later authority on the Bedouin, Wilfred Thesiger, in *Arabian Sands* (1959) described the role of the tribal chief thus: 'A Bedu sheikh has no paid retainers on whom he can rely to carry out his orders. He is merely the first among equals in a society where every man is intensely independent and quick to resent any hint of autocracy. His authority depends in consequence on the force of his own personality and his skill in handling men.'

A Bedouin has a natural sense of equality with his tribal chief, but also shows him an equally natural measure of reverence or respect, not least in his salutations. Any inadvertent discourtesy is frowned upon. There is a balance of traditional and largely unspoken mutual expectations, known to all, between the person in the role of tribal leader and the rest of the tribe.

Among free tribes of the Arabian desert until very recent times there was no taxation and the chiefs derived no revenues from their tribesmen. On the contrary, tribal leaders were expected to give generously from their comparatively greater wealth for the public benefit. Indeed the prestige of a tribal chief, as with any Bedouin, stemmed in part from his reputation for largesse. A Bedouin who beggared himself in generous hospitality to strangers could be revered.

It follows that the *shaykh* was expected to treat strangers with greater hospitality than other members of the tribe, to give to the extremely poor, to support widows and orphans, and to divide among his kinsmen whatever presents he received. To provide him with the wealth to fulfil this fatherly role of provider, the Bedouin chief in ancient times took a fourth part of the spoils of war and had the right to select for himself, before the division, some special gift, such as a young woman, camel or sword.

Among the Hebrew semi-nomadic tribes as recorded in the Bible we find much the same customs over dividing the spoils. Abraham and Jacob both led their tribesmen in battle. The tribal chief received a larger share of the booty (1 Samuel 30:20), including some choice gift (Judges 5:30, 8:24). Among the Semitic desert tribes some of the spoils of war, such as a weapon, were often set aside as votive offerings at some place sacred to tribal gods – a biblical example is the sword of Goliath which was hung at such a holy place (1 Samuel 21:9). Among the Hebrews, however, part of the chief's share of the booty was generally consecrated to God (Judges 8:27; 2 Samuel 8:10 f.; Micah 4:13) in addition to the fixed share assigned to the sanctuary in Levitical law (Numbers 31:28 ff.). Later, in Islam a similar provision was made. But even so the tribal chief had wealth to share generously with the needy or strangers when occasion presented itself. Much of his prestige, as I have said, depended on his reputation for open-handed hospitality.

Could there be a finer example of desert nomadic hospitality than that provided by Abraham when unexpectedly confronted with three visitors (Genesis 18:1–8)? He rushes from the opening of his tent to meet them and converts them into guests by begging them to enter his tent. He then hurries across to Sarah's tent and asks her to bake bread as quickly as she can. Next he runs to the cattle enclosure and chooses a tender calf for the servants to make ready for a feast. Finally, he stands over his guests at the ensuing meal and waits on them himself to make sure they are well served. Indeed, Arabic has a special word to sum up this elaborate and ceremonial solicitude accorded to visitors: it is *hafawah*, usually translated as 'to show honour to a guest'. A rabbinic legend has it that Abraham's tent had no less than four entrances so that a visitor approaching from any direction could be the more easily seen and pressed to enter as a guest. Clearly Abraham exemplified the virtue of generous hospitality to all-comers. He was a great leader in the nomadic tradition as well as being ancestor of both the Arab and the Jewish nations.

The principle of causality suggests that no effect can come before a cause – you cannot exist before your mother. It was self-evident to the Jews in the time of Jesus that their first 'cause' on earth – Abraham – must always be superior to any 'effects' – such as his descendants or 'children'. Any claim that Jesus, described by Matthew as a 'son of Abraham', was *greater* than Abraham himself would be met with scorn or derision. The early Christians, or some of them, did later assert that Jesus in heavenly form had pre-existed Abraham in time, and therefore that he was indeed the greater one (John 8:57–8), but this claim probably belongs to a time after the death of Jesus.

With the acceptance of Gentiles into the Christian church, the assumption that the divine promises made to Abraham were passed down like inherited land rights *solely* to his physical descendants in the lineage of Isaac and Jacob was challenged by Christians. Therefore a new leadership role for Abraham – apart from physically begetting a nation – had to be found. In the letters of the New Testament, Abraham begins to be presented as the father of the faithful in a moral sense, as the archetype and pattern of all righteousness and obedience. 'By faith Abraham obeyed when he was called to go out to a place which he was to receive as an inheritance; and he went out, not knowing

where he was to go' (Hebrews 11:8). *Lead* and *leader* come
from an old north European root word for a path, road, journey
or course of a ship at sea. Abraham did not have a clear idea
where his journey would lead him. He was willing to be led
himself by God on a journey into the unknown.

Here then is a new kind of leader, one who has a sense of
vocation from God and is prepared to undertake a journey without requiring to be told in advance where it will lead. He is
confident in God, and willing to take the risk. The early Christians saw here the prototype of a new relation between people
and God, seen as the leader of humanity. Their word for that
new relation was *faith*.

An ancient Aryan word, *God* functions both as general noun
god and as a proper name, *God* the creator. In the Common
or Proto-Semitic language which scholars believe to have once
existed, *El* functioned in exactly the same way: *el* was any god,
El was the Supreme God, patriarch of all the gods. It was *El*
that Abraham worshipped. The name appears in different guises
in the various Semitic languages without borrowing between
them. In Hebrew it is to be found in such names as Jacob's
sobriquet of *Isra-el*, he who strives or wrestles with God. The
early Arabic form was probably *ilah*, which gives us *Allah* (possibly with the help of the pronoun *el*, 'the' – 'the God'). In
Aramaic it is to be found in the words of Jesus on the cross
which begin *Eloi, Eloi* (my God, my God).

Assuming that the Semites had their origins in the deserts and
mountains of Arabia, the concept of *El* is best understood in that
context against that background. The immensity of the great sky,
arching above the solitary camel-rider, seems to emphasize the
greatness of God over humanity and all its other gods. *El* lives in
the tent of the heavens; he is Creator and Lord of all life. Here,
like a paramount tribal chief, *El* holds his *majlis* or council where
other lesser gods can have their say or make their requests known.
He is Lord of the desert; he owns it. Light is the beams from *El*'s
eyes; reality is what *El* thinks; creation is the result of his spoken
word or command. This Most High God alone is ultimately
worthy of worship. For he provides for his creatures. Who could
survive in that harsh desert environment without *El*?

Such was the concept of *El*, God, formed over centuries in the desert, perhaps the most barren environment in which humans have ever had to survive, one which leaves its indelible marks on the faces and bodies, character and spirit of those who lived in it as nomadic inhabitants. It remained in their folk memory long after they had exchanged their tents, woven from the black and brown hair of goats, for the stone-built houses of village and town.

When Semitic peoples such as the forebears of the Canaanite and Phoenician peoples migrated from the desert and settled down to agrarian life they added other gods to their existing tribal gods, ones that were reputed to have power over crops, fertility, weather, and the cycle of the year, in its never-ending pattern of death and rebirth. In this new environment the Most High God *El* lost status and ground to those other gods or *baals*. Among the Canaanites, for example, *El* remained but only as titular chief deity, still presiding in some of the Canaanite myths over his council of gods like divine tribal elders. But in these myths *El*, father of the gods and humanity, was overthrown by his son *Baal*, just as Zeus overthrew Chronos in Greek mythology. In the Phoenician cult, *El* also sinks to the status of a minor god among other *baals* (lords or gods), for the chief god of the Phoenicians (and their offshoot the Carthaginians) was Marduk – a god thirsty for human sacrifice.

Abraham's sense of a personal relationship with *El* the Supreme or Most High God, Creator and Lord of the earth, as if one was talking face to face with a friend, had the effect of producing something unique in a leader – humility. In Homer's *Iliad*, the Bible of the Greeks, humility is not to be found among the admired virtues. Pride or *hubris*, so often the central theme of Greek tragedy, marked or marred even the best of Greek leaders, as we have seen in the case of Alexander the Great. Even Themistocles and Pericles, two of the great Athenian leaders, fell prey to an arrogance stemming from pride in the end. Yet there is nothing proud or arrogant about Abraham. He is humility itself when, bowing low before God, he says, 'Behold, I have taken upon myself to speak to the Lord, I who am but dust and ashes' (Genesis 18:27).

Humility, from the Latin humus, means literally 'near the ground'. It is to be lowly, modest or meek. Meek is an old Norse word meaning soft, pliant, gentle. These words suggest someone who is without pride or self-will, gentle in nature and able to be guided by the lightest promptings of God in an entirely flexible way. The Hebrew word for humility, *hasne'a*, occurs only once in the Old Testament, in Micah (6:8):

> He has showed you, O man, what is good;
> and what does the Lord require of you
> but to do justice, and to love kindness,
> and to walk humbly with your God?

The cognate word in Arabic is *sana*, which suggests behaviour that is accommodating, flexible, yielding.

Humility, then, as we meet it for the first time here in the life and character of Abraham, is a reflex which comes from meeting God as if face to face. It is accompanied by an inward sensitivity and tractability to the will of God. It does not ask where the path will lead. It introduces a new theme in leadership, one that will appear again in the story of Jesus.

The Prophet – Moses

Moses was both the great national deliverer and the law-giver of the Hebrews. He is the prophet called by God to lead the confederation of twelve tribes out of Egypt, to preside over them as their leader during their decades of desert nomadic life, and then to lead them to their final destination – the land of Canaan. On its very threshold – on one of the mountains of Moab – Moses himself died. But the people continued their journey, passing over the Jordan and into the Promised Land.

At the time of Jesus' earthly life everyone believed that Moses was the actual author of the Pentateuch, as the first five books of the Hebrew scriptures which contain the Law are known. This belief made the name of Moses one of unrivalled authority. Like Abraham, he was seen not as a dead figure in the past, but as a living, if invisible, leader in the present – someone who shapes the course of daily life. The sect known as the Pharisees, for example, called themselves 'Moses' disciples' in contrast to those of Jesus; unlike the latter, they revered Moses and obeyed his written commands (John 9:28). As a second example, on the Mount of Transfiguration, three of Jesus' disciples had a vision of Jesus conferring with Moses and Elijah as equals, as if they were both very much alive and concerned with the affairs of their people. Eventually and perhaps symbolically, Moses and Elijah faded from their view, leaving 'Jesus alone' in their sight.

The role of Moses in the story of Israel is comparable to the role of the prophet Muhammad in Islam. A *prophet*, the Greek word that translates the Hebrew and Arabic *nabi*, means literally one who declares God's will before all. A prophet may predict events – many do – but prophecy is wider than that. A prophet is a spokesman, one inspired to speak for God. For the Jews, as a prophet Moses could have no equal. The Pentateuch itself declared as much in its closing words: 'And there has not arisen a prophet since in Israel like Moses, whom the Lord knew face to face' (Deuteronomy 34:10).

According to tradition only available to us in the Bible, Moses was born to parents of the tribe of Levi. As the Egyptians were then killing Hebrew male babies to keep the numbers down, his mother is said to have hidden him in a basket among the reeds by the Nile. Pharaoh's daughter, the Exodus account goes, found and adopted him, giving him an Egyptian name, Moses, meaning 'one drawn out of the water'.

When Moses became a young man, he was increasingly drawn to his own people: he visited them frequently and saw their burdens. One day he came across an Egyptian overseer beating a Hebrew mercilessly. Having checked no one was in sight, Moses killed the Egyptian and buried his body in the sand. Next day he found two Hebrews who were fighting each other. 'Why do you strike your fellow?' he asked the aggressor, having pulled them apart. 'Who made you a leader and judge over us?' the man replied. 'Do you mean to kill me as you killed the Egyptian?'

The fellow's words aroused a sudden panic in Moses, for he knew now that the murder he had committed the day before would soon be common knowledge. Fearing for his life, Moses fled to the land of Midian which lay on the far eastern side of the Sinai desert astride what is now the Gulf of Aqaba.

Once in the land of Midian, Moses came to the aid of some girls whose attempts to water their family flock at a well was being disrupted by other shepherds. The girls proved to be the seven daughters of 'the priest of Midian', Jethro. These Midianities were yet another Semitic semi-nomadic people: a wandering band of them had bought Joseph from his brothers and sold him into slavery in Egypt. In fact they were more nomads than town dwellers, for in battle they were camel-riders (Judges 7:12), which suggests that they grazed their herds deep within the desert like the camel-based pure Bedouin tribes of later times. Moses may have felt at home with Jethro and his kinsfolk because, in all probability, they worshipped the paramount God *El.*

Jethro gave Moses hospitality in his tents, and eventually a daughter, Zipporah, in marriage. She bore him two sons, Gershon and Eliezer. For several years, then, Moses lived in exile the life of a shepherd among this nomadic people.

In the solitude of the wilderness while minding his father-in-law's flock of sheep, Moses heard God's call: he was to return and lead God's people, 'the sons of Israel', out of the oppressive slavery of Egypt. Their destination would be a 'land flowing with milk and honey', the Promised Land where the Canaanites presently lived (Exodus 3:1–10). As a leader, however, Moses was aware that he lacked one apparently necessary gift – he could not speak well in public. He was not articulate or fluent with words, nor persuasive in the debates of a council – vital skills for a leader. As Moses expressed it to God: 'I am slow of speech and of tongue' (4:10). But God commanded him not to be anxious on that score. God himself would, he assured him 'be with your mouth and teach you what you shall speak' (4:12). Moreover, God added, Moses' brother Aaron, who was a natural speaker, would act as his interpreter. Indeed, when Moses returned to Egypt and met the 'elders', the tribal chiefs of the Hebrews in council, it was Aaron's eloquent presentation of Moses' vision and plan that won their assent.

If God calls a person to be a leader of his people, the story seems to teach us, God makes it possible for him or her to fulfil that vocation. An apparently missing ability may be developed – Moses became an effective public speaker later on in the story. God uses others, too, to complement the weaknesses of a leader with their own strengths. For no one person has all the gifts necessary for leading a large body of people.

Nor does God seem over-impressed with visible physical qualities, such as height or strength. God looks inward on the 'heart' – a person's inner spirit. It is possible, for example, that Moses may not have had the physical badge of having been circumcised, and so by that criterion he was not technically a Jew. Circumcision was common among all Semitic peoples and indeed in the ancient world at large, but it became more specifically associated with being a Jew. Moses' apparent lack of circumcision can be deduced from a curious incident during the journey of his return to Egypt (Exodus 4:24–6). In the story, oddly, God pursues Moses 'and sought to kill him'. But Zipporah circumcises their small son with a flint and touches Moses with the blood, after which God lets Moses alone. Perhaps later editors felt it necessary to accredit Moses with at least a symbolic form of the outward badge of Jewish manhood.

One has the impression that it is God who is leading Israel, and that Moses is the very human and fallible instrument by which he does so. As we have seen, Moses is no orator. He is afraid to stand up to Pharaoh and his magicians; nor can he bring himself to believe that the Hebrews will accept him as their leader. He loses his temper, and is indecisive when the Israelites blame both him and God for bringing them into the desert to die of thirst. Continually God has to strengthen his confidence, working miracle after miracle to prove that his power is at work in and through Moses, and reprimanding him for his lack of trust. God's agents, it seems, do not necessarily have to have natural gifts, merely a willingness to offer themselves and to be guided by God. But God never abandons those whom he has called to his service.

How far the account given in Exodus accords with what really happened in history is a matter for the historians. But, from a leadership perspective, some parts of the story do ring true. For example, when the Israelites proved reluctant to exchange the known discomforts of Egypt for the unknown hardships of surviving in the desert, Moses wisely set them only a *limited objective*: he invited them to move into the Sinai desert for just three days in order to worship at Mount Horeb. Sometimes the most difficult task for a leader is to overcome the inertia of a large body of people, their reluctance to embrace change. By offering the Israelites what we would call a 'return ticket', Moses and Aaron achieved their first aim, which was to get the tribes moving eastwards. But while they looked over their shoulders, especially in times of extreme difficulty, it was never easy to keep them moving forwards. An Australian Aborigine proverb says, *If you look back you will never go.*

Later, after the Israelites had abandoned any thoughts of returning to Egypt and settled down to their nomadic life in the desert, Moses gave them the elements of what we know as the Law (Hebrew, *Torah*). Although the Law of Moses incorporated much of the existing tribal law and tradition, it was centred upon the concept that Israel – the new nation forged from the tribes in the desert heat – had been called to be the servant of God. Israel was to be a dedicated nation, holy and pure before God. Such was the vision of Moses. But, as T. S. Eliot was to write much later:

> Between the idea
> And the Reality
> Between the motion
> And the act
> Falls the Shadow

About this time the tetragrammaton YHWH, a name so holy it could not be uttered, came into use as a proper name for God. The earliest form of it may have been *Yh* or *Yah*, possible a name for a desert god of thunder and volcanoes, or perhaps a tribal war-god. Whatever the origin, *Yah* or *Yahweh* became more and more identified with *El*. One interpretation of the prophet Elijah's name, for example, is '*El* is my *Yah*,' while the name Joel does mean '*Yah* is *El*'. The Lord, as this composite

God is called, dwells among his people and acts as their leader. His authority, too, underwrites the simple but comprehensive code at the heart of the Mosaic Law that we know as the Ten Commandments. The story tells us that God revealed this law directly to Moses, together with its supporting framework of rules, regulations and policies.

Moses also acted as the principal judge in administering the new code which the tribes slowly came to accept. Wisdom as a judge is a path to leadership in a tribal society. But as the numbers of those coming to Moses for arbitration or judgment increased so the toll on Moses' time became ever greater. As the following story reveals, whatever his shortcomings may have been as a leader Moses showed himself possessed of one great strength: he was willing to listen to advice and act upon it if it was sound.

Jethro, the priest of the Midianites, paid a visit to his son-in-law in the desert encampment of the Israelites. He observed that Moses was over-working himself hearing the various cases brought before him. From his father-in-law Moses learnt a key lesson in the art of being a strategic leader – the leader of a large body of people. We call it delegation.

On the morrow Moses sat to judge the people, and the people stood about Moses from morning till evening. When Moses' father-in-law saw all that he was doing for the people, he said, 'What is this that you are doing for the people? Why do you sit alone, and all the people stand about you from morning till evening?' And Moses said to his father-in-law, 'Because the people come to me to inquire of God; when they have a dispute, they come to me and I decide between a man and his neighbour . . .' Moses' father-in-law said to him, 'What you are doing is not good. You and the people with you will wear yourselves out, for the thing is too heavy for you; you are not able to perform it alone. Listen now to my voice; I will give you counsel, and God be with you! You shall represent the people before God, and bring their cases to God; and you shall teach them the statutes and the decisions, and make them know the way in which they must walk and what they must do. Moreover choose able men from all the people, such as fear God, men who are trustworthy and who hate a bribe; and place such men over the people as rulers of thousands, of hundreds, of fifties, and of tens. And let them judge the people at all times; every great matter they shall bring to you, but any small matter they shall decide themselves; so it will be easier for you, and they will bear the burden with you. If you do this, and God so commands you, then you will be able to endure, and all this people also will go to their place in peace.' (Exodus 18:13–23)

Another small step which reveals Moses' organizational ability was the appointment of administrative or executive officers, attached to tribal chiefs (Deuteronomy 16:18–19; 20:5, 9). They were known in Hebrew as *shoterim*, the same word as is used in Exodus to describe the Hebrew overseers or foremen of Pharaoh's slave-gangs whose task it was to ensure that the right number of bricks were produced daily (Exodus 5:10). Some of the Hebrews may have wondered on occasion if they had found freedom in the desert, or merely exchanged one pharaoh for another!

Although Moses doubtlessly did decide to step back from the day-to-day judicial work in the way Jethro suggested, the picture given in Exodus 18 of him appointing the leaders of Israel – the 'rulers' over thousands, hundreds, fifties and tens – is probably more idealistic than historical. This decimal military organization almost certainly belongs to a later age. The tribal chiefs, the equivalent of the Bedouin *shaykhs*, not only led their kinsmen into battle but also were accustomed to act as judges. They met together in council to take any important decisions that affected the whole confederation. Moses' leadership existed, so to speak, alongside this tribal order. The source of it was, of course, his direct relation with God as the prophet. He must have acquired great personal prestige, so that his influence in the government's direction of affairs within the tribal confederation was usually decisive.

As a leader, Moses must have been extremely formidable, especially when blazing with righteous anger. But for much of the time that volcano was silent. The humility and meekness of

Moses became a byword. He was 'very meek, more than all men that were on the face of the earth' (Numbers 12:3). Yet, as with Abraham, it was the meekness of a spirited horse responsive to its rider's lightest touch. Moses never lost the sense of being a servant. Despite a strength of character that grew over years, Moses was always intent that Israel should serve God, not himself. It is as if his message to the fledgling nation of Israel, delivered both by word and example, was simply: 'God is your leader, not me.'

Moses showed his practical wisdom as a leader by choosing as his successor a man very different from himself, one with the experience and skills of a military leader necessary for the invasion of Canaan that lay ahead – Joshua, son of Nun, of the tribe of Ephraim. He was chosen by Moses to be 'one who shall go out before them and come in before them, who shall lead them out and bring them in; that the congregation of the Lord may not be as sheep which have no shepherd' (Numbers 27:17). The Greek form of Joshua, which meant in Hebrew roughly 'God helps', is the name Jesus which Joseph and Mary gave their eldest son.

After the death of Moses 'the servant of the Lord', God told Joshua to cross over the Jordan into the Promised Land. He promised Joshua that 'as I was with Moses, so I will be with you; I will not fail you or forsake you. . . . Be strong and of good courage; be not frightened, neither be dismayed; for the Lord your God is with you wherever you go' (Joshua 1:5, 9). There speaks God the Leader.

The Shepherd-King – David

It was the prophet Samuel who chose David from among the sons of Jesse to be anointed king. As the youngest of them he was looking after the family's flock of sheep when summoned by his father to meet Samuel. Doubtless Samuel was impressed by the fact that this boy had the spirit to fight lions and bears to save the sheep entrusted to him. In the famous encounter that followed he slew Goliath with his shepherd's sling.

After Saul, whom Samuel had anointed as Judah's first king,

fell in battle, all the tribes of Israel came to David at Hebron and said, 'Behold, we are your bone and flesh. In times past, when Saul was king over us, it was you that led out and brought in Israel; and the Lord God said to you, "You shall be shepherd of my people Israel, and you shall be prince over Israel"' (2 Samuel 5:1–2). After making a covenant or agreement with the tribal leaders of the people before the Lord at Hebron, they anointed David king over Israel. David was thirty years old when he began to reign, and he reigned forty years. The Psalmist (78:70–2) summed up his vocation in these words:

> He chose David his servant,
>   and took him from the sheepfolds;
> from tending the ewes that had young he brought him
>   to be the shepherd of Jacob his people,
> of Israel his inheritance.
> With upright heart he tended them,
>   and guided them with skilful hand.

Diversion: The Example of the Shepherd

It is clear from this passage that probably the strongest biblical metaphor for a leader is that of the *shepherd*. Classical authors such as Homer and Xenophon had used the same image too, but it is not so prominent in their writings as it is in the Bible. Given our present knowledge of leadership it is a singularly rich image. For we know now that someone in a leadership role has three core and overlapping functions: to achieve the task, to hold a group together as a unity, and to meet individual needs. We know also, as I have already said, that leadership is essentially a journey word. Putting these two insights together may help us to understand why the shepherd metaphor is so fertile in overtones and implications: it is a simple and serviceable model for a future leader, even though many of the lessons would have been more implicit than explicit.

The shepherd gave direction to the flock by leading it from the front, sometimes walking for up to twenty miles a day, in search of the sparse grass that grows in the wilderness. For even 'the pastures of the wilderness' (Psalms 65:12; John 2:22) were welcome in the spring, when the desert is green with fresh grass and flowers that will burn up in the summer heat. Lambs naturally follow their mothers and fully grown wild sheep who live in bands follow their dominant ram. To mark their paths, sheep have hoof-glands which give off scent. Early humans in the Mediterranean basin at least at long ago as 6000 BC observed this phenomenon and saw that sheep could be tamed and induced to follow a human leader instead of a ram. Shepherds in the hill-country and in the wilderness of Judaea had dogs, but they were fierce mastiffs kept to protect their flocks of sheep and goats, and not used to round them up or drive them.

As a rule, the shepherd goes before the flock, but not infrequently he is seen behind it. The shepherd walks behind, especially in the evening when the flock is on its way to the fold, in order that he may gather the stragglers and protect them from the stealthy wolf. The shepherd also often walks by the side of the flock, somewhere around the middle of the straggling line. In the case of large flocks the chief shepherd goes before, and the under-shepherd or helper brings up the rear.

Keeping the flock close together was essential for their safety. No shepherd would go so far ahead as to lose sight or be out of earshot of his sheep. The natural instinct of predators, such as wolves and hyenas, was to scatter the flock and then kill their individual victims. Therefore the unity or cohesiveness of the flock was important to the shepherd. If he saw a sheep or goat wandering off, he called it back; should it still walk away, he hurled a stone from his sling, so as to fall just beyond it and send it scurrying back to the flock. If a sheep became lost 'on the hills' (Matthew 18:12), in the hills and gullies of the Judaean wilderness, the shepherd had to decide whether or not to leave the flock in order to go in search of it. If several shepherds had charge of the flock it was easier for one to go off on his own, but even so his departure would weaken the collective strength of the shepherds. For the main threat to the flock came more from armed raiders rather than from the small mountain panthers or leopards, lions, bears, jackals, hyenas and wolves, which roamed in Judaea in biblical days.

The shepherd, then, came to personify unity. Hence the proverbial saying in the Bible: *Smite the shepherd and the sheep will be scattered*. In order to keep their flocks safe and together at night, a time of greater danger, shepherds often herded them into the limestone caves which abound in the Judaean hills, or they made sheepfolds with dry stone walls. In desert areas, where stones could not be found, they constructed their folds from thorn bushes. Wolves sometimes defied the dogs and leapt over these barriers, and so the shepherd might keep some of the lambs and young kids close to his tent for the night. 'O fairest among women,' sings the author of the Song of Solomon (1:8), 'follow in the tracks of the flock, and pasture your kids beside the shepherds' tents.'

Flocks in Judaea are often composed of sheep and goats, which are much more unruly than sheep alone. Goats tend to be black while sheep in contrast are white, so they are easy to distinguish at a distance. Goats are especially fond of nibbling young leaves but will eat scrub, whereas sheep prefer the fresh short grass if they can find it. But sheep and goats in mixed flocks do not always co-exist happily and the shepherd must work to keep them together harmoniously. This characteristic made it often necessary to separate the goats from the sheep in the fold. In all human groups and organizations there are similar tendencies to internal divisiveness.

The perpetual journeys of the shepherd and his flock brought danger and hardship for both of them. The shepherd shared these dangers on an equal footing with his sheep. He carried no more than a bag or wallet, together with a staff and sling. The summer sun burnt both of them by day, both shivered in the winter snows and icy winds. Both man and sheep ran the risk of attacks by wild animals or of treading on deadly vipers that lurked in the limestone rocks. It is not hard to believe that the shepherds came to love their charges; each could be recognized individually and called by name. Therefore it is not surprising that the Israelites applied the metaphor of the caring shepherd to God. The Twenty-Third Psalm is the song of a 'sheep' whose every need has been met by God the shepherd.

Like all analogies, the metaphor of the shepherd-and-sheep

for leaders of people does break down eventually. People and sheep obviously differ in a number of important respects. But the broad functions of leadership are contained in the image. The shepherd is responding to three kinds of implicit needs present in the flock: they need to find food and so he leads them on the path to their desired destination; he holds them together in cohesive and harmonious unity; and lastly, he meets their individual needs. He knows each sheep or goat by name. He makes sure that it finds the right food and enough water. He anoints an individual sheep's thorn-wounds with oil. He tends a sick animal until it recovers its strength.

A joyful moment would come at sunset when the shepherd who had led out the flock of sheep in the morning brought them all safely back to the safe fold. For it is one thing to lead people out on a journey, but it is another thing to bring them safely home. That analogy holds good for all forms of leadership. The successful military leader, for example, is the one who brings his army home in safety and, if victorious in triumph, to a great welcome, with all the joys and celebrations of such a homecoming. For soldiers in all ages there is no sweeter experience.

Both Moses and David had worked as shepherds, and the implication is that some of the qualities and skills learnt there are transferable to the leadership of people and ultimately to the nation. David guided the human flock entrusted to him by God 'with skilful hand'. It is difficult not to believe that in his youth, Jesus had also the care of the family's and neighbours' sheep and goats among the hills of Galilee, for the imagery of the shepherd informs his teaching on leadership.

The Greek word for 'good' in the saying attributed to Jesus, 'I am the good shepherd' (John 10:14), is *kalos*, meaning skilful, as opposed to *agathos*, which means morally good. A good shepherd-leader masters the skills of leadership; he knows his business. He is no hireling who will run away at the first hint of danger; if need be, he will lay down his life for his sheep entrusted to him.

The vision of a flock of sheep without a shepherd becomes the most powerful image in the Bible for the need for a leader.

It is this perception of need which is the means whereby God calls a person to become a leader or shepherd. Moses had responded himself to that call, and in due course he appointed as his successor Joshua, a man with the spirit in him as one 'who shall go out before them and come in before them, who shall lead them out and bring them in; that the congregation of the Lord may not be as sheep which have no shepherd' (Numbers 27:17).

Sheep need care and protection from their shepherds, but humans need something more from their leaders – inspiration. Clearly David was an inspirational leader. A hint of David's gift for leadership in this respect is given in the following story. The setting for it is the guerrilla warfare before David became king, waged against the Philistines who then controlled the western parts of the land of Canaan. David's forces were led by thirty 'mighty men', his chosen captains.

> Three of the thirty chief men went down to the rock to David at the cave of Adullam, when the army of Philistines was encamped in the valley of Rephaim. David was then in the stronghold; and the garrison of the Philistines was then at Bethlehem. And David said longingly, 'O that some one would give me water to drink from the well of Bethlehem which is by the gate!' Then the three mighty men broke through the camp of the Philistines, and drew water out of the well of Bethlehem which was by the gate, and took and brought it to David. But David would not drink of it; he poured it out to the Lord, and said, 'Far be it from me before my God that I should do this. Shall I drink the lifeblood of these men? For at the risk of their lives they brought it.' Therefore he would not drink it. (1 Chronicles 11:15–19)

That three of David's captains should be willing to risk their lives to surprise him with a drink of water from the well of Bethlehem, doubtless the very well where his mother had drawn water for him while he was growing up there, speaks volumes about his ability to inspire others. The poet in David saw the water they brought as symbolic of the lifeblood they had been willing to shed for him. Then he had poured it all out on to the ground as a libation with a simple prayer to God. The story of a drink refused in this way reminds us of Alexander the Great (pages 17–18), but David's motives were different and reflected his deep awe of God. The whole of David's spirit is captured in a nutshell in this story.

A good shepherd, we have seen, creates unity. One of David's greatest achievements was to create a city in the middle of his kingdom which would be a centre and symbol of unity for God's nation – Jerusalem. Following the analogy a step further, the walled city of Jerusalem would become the spiritual sheepfold of God's flock. David's commander Joab, acting on his orders, stormed and captured this Jebusite city which lay roughly in the centre of the hill-country that formed the spine of the land of Canaan. It was here that David based his government and the headquarters of his largely mercenary army – he even had Philistines serving in his bodyguard. The Ark of the Covenant was brought to the city with great ceremony (2 Samuel 6:1–19). Thus 'the city of David' became the religious as well as the civic and military capital of land. David planned to build a 'house of cedar' to house more permanently the sacred chest with the tablets on which were inscribed the Law of Moses. The site he had in mind was on the plateau of the hill immediately above the city. He had bought the land from one of the Jebusite inhabitants, named Araunah; it included a bare expanse of rock originally used as a threshing floor and possibly as a 'high place' for sacrifices. The historic rock is still visible today under the graceful, golden Dome of the Rock built by Muslims in the sixth century AD.

In fact David was more like a *nasi* or prince – what Arabs today would call an *amir* or a *sultan* – than a king (in Arabic *malik*) in the full sense. It was not David himself but his son Solomon by Bathsheba who would receive symbols we associate with a king: crown, throne and sceptre. After Solomon was solemnly anointed and crowned by Zadok the chief priest at the Gihon spring, where the Ark was kept in the Tent of Gathering, he then led a procession up to the palace in the city accompanied by the sounds of trumpets, clapping and cries of 'Long live the

King!' The act of ascending the steps to the throne and sitting on it in the royal palace would come to symbolize kingly rule. David, by contrast, had no such coronation. It is true that he was anointed, but by the tribal chiefs and elders and not by the chief priest.

David, then, is a transitional figure. He stands between the age when Israel was still a group of semi-nomad tribes and the age when it became a state with the settled institutions of monarchy, taxes and administration. As former dwellers in the long low 'houses of hair' – the black tents woven from goat and camel hair – the Israelites had always been adverse to monarchy. For they had been as free as the desert wind. Only the crisis of a war against the Philistines that seemed to threaten their very existence had led the tribal leaders to petition Samuel to appoint a king (1 Samuel 8:4–5), and what they had in mind was a paramount ruler who would rule with their consent and support. In David's long reign they became accustomed to such a *nasi* or 'mighty prince' leading them in battle but also living in some state in a palace in Jerusalem, with courtiers, officials and a large harem, not to mention a standing professional army. All of these innovations cost money. Yet taxation, the inevitable accompaniment of central government, was deeply unpopular then as now. Towards the end of David's reign (973 BC), a royal commission headed by Joab was appointed to carry out a census of the people (2 Samuel 24; 1 Chronicles 21) in order the better to tax them. It was followed by a plague and it occasioned great resentment among the people.

Not that these negative aspects of the reign lingered in the popular mind. In his forty years as God's under-shepherd, David imprinted himself for ever in the collective memory of the Jews. It was a story of unequalled success. His generals defeated the Philistines to the west and the Canaanites to the north; they struck east and south against aggressive neighbours on these borders. Even the Aramaeans far to the north were subdued and their capital at Damascus taken. To match these victories on the frontiers in Jerusalem, important and far-reaching reforms were undertaken in the institutions of government and the foundations of an enduring state were laid.

In 2 Samuel 7 we read that the prophet Nathan gave David a promise that his dynasty would rule for ever. In fact David's 'house' lasted some four centuries in the south, but after Solomon's death the northern tribes had established their own line of kings with their capital in the city of Samaria, and so Israel was split into two kingdoms. Yet Nathan's prophecy formed the seed of the hope than one day the 'house' of David would be restored by a 'shoot' from the family, 'a root of Jesse' (David's father), a person who in the course of time was seen to be supernatural. It is my view that the chief prophecy to this effect (Isaiah 11:1) is directly or indirectly the most likely source of Jesus' Aramaic surname – *Nazara* or *Nazarene*. For 'shoot' in Hebrew and Aramaic is *nazar* (see Note 1).

Above all, David – tall, handsome and with 'beautiful eyes' – acquired a remarkable charisma that to some extent survived his death. No single individual in the story of Israel had ever so combined all the qualities and virtues of a shepherd-leader. To David's genius as a leader must be added his gifts as a musician and poet. It is not so surprising, then, that David became to the Jews of later history what Achilles was to the ancient Greeks.

'Not everything that King David did, on the ground, or the rooftops is acceptable to a Jew, or is something I like.' When the Foreign Minister of modern Israel, Simon Peres, uttered these words in the Knesset (Parliament) in 1994 they caused a riot among the orthodox Jewish members, and votes of no confidence in him were passed. By his reference to 'rooftops' Peres was, of course, referring to the story of Bathsheba (2 Samuel 11–12). David had coveted Bathsheba the moment that from the vantage point of a rooftop he had seen her bathing below. He sent her husband, one of his mercenary captains named Uriah the Hittite, to be killed in the front line of battle so that he could make her his wife. Yet after the stern rebuke of Nathan the prophet, given as a parable, David was genuinely penitent. King though he was, David could take just criticism from God through the lips of his prophet – a sign of both integrity and humility.

It is these qualities – integrity and humility – that make David stand out head and shoulders above all the kings of Judah and

Israel. They blended – sometimes uncomfortably – with his passionate intensity as a human being. Who can forget his love for Saul's son Jonathan or his heartrending grief after the death of his rebellious son Absalom?

When Samuel broke the news to Saul that God intended to replace him as king (1 Samuel 13:14), he added: 'The Lord has sought out *a man after his own heart*.' Perhaps these six simple words are the true epitaph for Israel's first and greatest king.

3

The Chief Rulers in Jesus' Day

Where there is no vision, the people perish.
Proverbs 29:18 (AV)

The great leaders of the Bible – such as Abraham and Moses, David and Elijah – were not, I have suggested, seen as figures of history but more as invisible contemporaries. Indeed, to many Jews in the days of Jesus, they must have seemed more real as national leaders than the actual people who held positions of authority over the community of Israel or some part of it. For these national 'shepherds' were an indifferent lot.

Three of these figures in particular must have seemed to the common people either remote or alien or both – Caiaphas the chief priest, Herod Antipas and Pontius Pilate. Each of them would set eyes on Jesus in the last days of his life, although whether or not there was any real meeting of minds is much more debatable. It could be argued, however, that none of them was a *leader* in the true sense of the word, merely a ruler or governor, and therefore that technically they have no place in this book. Still, it is interesting to reflect on the model of authority that each represented, in contrast to the leadership of the man who would one day stand before them meekly, like a sheep about to be led out to the place of slaughter.

The Chief Priest – Caiaphas

When Jesus was at work the chief or high priest (both translations of the Greek word *archihierus*) was Caiaphas, who held office from AD 18 to 37. An ossuary with an Aramaic inscription which appears to read 'Joseph, son of Caiaphas' was found near Jerusalem in 1990, thus most probably identifying the family tomb.

Caiaphas was the son-in-law of Annas, who had been high priest between AD 10 and 15. Although deposed by the Romans, Annas continued to hold an influential position in the Sanhedrin and among the select number of high priestly families in Jerusalem – the families from whom chief priests could be chosen. According to John's Gospel, it was Annas who presided over the preliminary hearing of the case against Jesus immediately after his arrest and prior to the trial by Caiaphas. No fewer than six members of Annas' family served as high priests during the Herodian period.

The chief priest, as successor to Aaron, had a leading role in the Temple cult. For example, he alone entered the 'Holy of Holies', the innermost chamber of the Temple, on *Yom Kippur*, the Day of Atonement. Dressed in the bejewelled full regalia, a blue robe with gold bells and tassels over his white linen tunic, he walked through a cloud of incense into the sanctuary, while outside a bullock was sacrificed and its blood sprinkled on the mercy seat. As part of the ritual, two goats were brought forward. One was chosen by lot for sacrifice and the other – bearer of the nation's sins which the high priest had transferred to it – was released to wander in the Judaean wilderness which stretched away from the Mount of Olives to the Dead Sea, some fifteen miles away and some 2000 feet below sea level.

Josephus had coined a word for the Jewish form of government – a *theocracy* – but in fact, like that of Rome before the emperors, it was an oligarchy. A small number of aristocratic families, with those having the right to provide the high priests at their core, provided what leadership Israel as a nation now possessed. The office of chief priest does bear some superficial resemblance to today's elected president of a republic – though the chief priest was chosen by a small coterie of aristocratic families in the bloodline of Aaron and without a hint of democracy as we know it today. But, in times of emergency, when an official representative of the nation was needed to speak on its behalf, the chief priest alone had the necessary authority. The Greek and Roman overlords recognized this fact by conferring on the chief priests – or at least the ones they approved of – the title of *ethnarch*, leader of the people.

In other words, the chief priest was the nearest that Israel now came to having its own *nasi* or 'prince'. The highly priestly office, never intended for the purpose, had to take on a political function. Like the old tribal paramount chief or king, for example, the chief priest was now the chief judge in Israel. As in Islam, the Mosaic Law made no real distinction between civil and religious cases. The Roman governors, following Roman practice, allowed the Jews full autonomy when it came to their own laws and customs. They did, however, reserve certain crimes for their own jurisdiction, notably sedition or rebellion.

There was one relic of the old desert days when the tribal chiefs met in council as the confederation's highest authority – the Sanhedrin. Like a *nasi* or 'prince', the high priest was expected to lead with the advice and consent of the 'elders'. In the days of Jesus this traditional body of the successors to the tribal leaders had become known by the Greek name for a council, *sunedrion*. Yet it still numbered about seventy members, the number traditionally said to have been instituted by Moses in the Sinai desert. But we have already encountered the tribal council in the days when the Hebrew tribes lived and worked more or less as slaves in Egypt.

As political institutions, however, both the office of chief priest and the Sanhedrin had been much diminished. Roman overlordship was a heavy yoke to wear for a proud and haughty nation. Herod the Great, the puppet of the Romans, had looked upon both high priest and Sanhedrin as allies of his deadly rivals for supreme power – the Hasmonaeans, also known as the Maccabees. Led by Matthias (166 BC), they had seized power in the war against the successors of Alexander the Great and their Jewish allies who sought to Hellenize the Jews and their distinctive religion. The sons of Matthias – Judas, Jonathan and Simon – had led the long and bitter war against the Seleucids. The Seleucids, who ruled Syria, were descendants of the captain of Alexander's bodyguard, Seleucus, who, like Alexander, had in the course of time declared himself to be a living god. From Simon's time (142 BC) the Hasmonaeans reigned over Judaea until 63 BC, but they were far from being model rulers.

The fact that the Hasmonaean kings tended also to serve as

high priests contributed to the politicization of the high priestly office. When Herod the Great seized Jerusalem in 37 BC and under Roman patronage became king, he did what he could to weaken the authority of both chief priest and Sanhedrin. Yet even Herod could not do away with these institutions, and he had to live with them as best he could. The Romans followed suit, but they took upon themselves the right to approve the high priest chosen by the family heads before his appointment or to dismiss him – as happened to Annas – if they did not like what he did or said. The fact that Caiaphas lasted nineteen years as high priest speaks volumes for his acceptability to the Romans or his political skills.

By Jesus' day the Sanhedrin's membership consisted of three segments: the representatives of high priestly families, the elders and the scribes. But in practice these elements were far from distinct. For example, the elders (the heirs to the tribal leaders), known in Greek as *presbuteroi*, and the high priestly families had become so intermarried that it was hard to distinguish between the lay *archontes* (rulers) and the Aaronic priestly aristocracy who controlled the key office of high priest.

The third element of the Sanhedrin's membership was provided by the scribes, the important class of learned Jews who devoted themselves to the study of the Law of Moses and the associated traditions. Some of them made its exposition their professional occupation, though others would support themselves by working in a trade. The English word *scribe* translate the Greek *grammateis*, the learned ones. In the Gospels, the scribes are also called 'lawyers' or 'doctors of the law'.

The important thing about the scribes is that they provided the intellectual leadership of the Jews, such as it was. For in that Semitic cultural context the only intellectual field open for men of outstanding intelligence – arguably a national trait of the Jews – was the study of the scriptures. The scribes were predecessors of the *rabbis*. In Hebrew *rabbi* meant originally 'my great one', ('sir' or 'master' in English), but it eventually became a religious title. After the destruction of Jerusalem in AD 70, when the Sanhedrin was reconvened in Galilee, it was composed entirely of rabbis, their president adopting for himself the old Hebrew and Aramaic name of *nasi*, leader. When Bar-Kochba, 'son of a star', led the last revolt against Rome in AD 132, Rabbi Akaba and others hailed him as the Messiah. On his coins Bar-Kochba is called 'Prince (*Nasi*) of Israel'.

The scribes in the time of Jesus tended to be members of parties or sects defined by their broad attitude to the Mosaic Law. The origins of the Pharisees as a sect go back to the early days of the Maccabean rebellion. They were the liberals in the sense that they used the existence of an oral tradition in order to interpret the written Mosaic Law. Their intention in so doing was to make the Law more completely and readily obeyable in the conditions and circumstances of the day. They sought *national* obedience to the Law as their chief end. They were leaders in the sense that they moved among the people in order to persuade the people – by precept if not always by example – to observe the Law of Moses. And it is clear that, despite a largely unfavourable image in the Christian Gospels, the people as a whole did respond to their leadership, for the rabbis who led the nation after AD 70 were largely drawn from the Pharisaic persuasion.

The other main party were the Sadducees. They were in the minority as membership seems to have been limited to the more aristocratic families in Jerusalem. Traditionalists in faith and practice, the Sadducees stressed a strict adherence to the written Law. They were especially strict about the ritual ordinances that governed the Temple cult. They believed that practising their traditional religion in this way could be accommodated with living under Roman rule, and they were opposed to any attempts to change the status quo.

The Sadducees also rejected the doctrine of 'the resurrection of the dead' which they held to be an innovation. The Pharisees, however, had espoused it. Paul of Tarsus – a Pharisee by background – cleverly exploited that difference of opinion to stir up a dissension between the two factions when he found himself on trial before the Sanhedrin.

And Paul, looking intently at the council, said, 'Brethren, I have lived before God in all good conscience up to this day.'

And the high priest Ananias commanded those who stood by him to strike him on the mouth. Then Paul said to him, 'God shall strike you, you whitewashed wall! Are you sitting to judge me according to the law, and yet contrary to the law you order me to be struck?' Those who stood by said, 'Would you revile God's high priest?' And Paul said, 'I did not know, brethren, that he was the high priest; for it is written, "You shall not speak evil of a ruler of your people."'

But when Paul perceived that one part were Sadducees and the other Pharisees, he cried out in the council, 'Brethren, I am a Pharisee, a son of Pharisees; with respect to the hope and the resurrection of the dead I am on trial.' And when he had said this, a dissension arose between the Pharisees and the Sadducees; and the assembly was divided. For the Sadducees say that there is no resurrection, nor angel, nor spirit; but the Pharisees acknowledge them all. Then a great clamour arose; and some of the scribes of the Pharisees' party stood up and contended, 'We find nothing wrong in this man. What if a spirit or an angel spoke to him?' And when the dissension became violent, the tribune, afraid that Paul would be torn in pieces by them, commanded the soldiers to go down and take him by force from among them and bring him into the barracks. (Acts 23:1–10)

This account gives us a vivid glimpse into the Sanhedrin at work. Notice how the high priest's office is held in great respect, even by Paul.

In fact the chief priest of the day, the Jerusalem noble families and the Sanhedrin had a difficult path to tread. They had to maintain their national and religious identity on the one hand, while on the other hand managing relations with their Roman overlords in order to exploit whatever flexibility there was in the system. Until the Jerusalem oligarchy lost control in the period leading up to the Jewish Revolt, they discharged this leadership responsibility reasonably well. The Jews enjoyed all the advantages of the *Pax Romana* and received some unique privileges, such as exemption from military service. Above all, they were allowed to practise their religion without interference.

The growing numbers of the *diaspora* (Greek for 'dispersion'), as the Jews scattered round the world outside Palestine were known, also benefited from Roman peace. They flourished and could now be found in every city (John 7:35). In the larger centres, such as Alexandria, the Jews occupied their own quarter with its synagogues under the rule of elders and rabbis. In Rome itself, for example, the forty to fifty thousand Jews were not required to serve in the legions, had their own courts, were permitted to collect money for the Temple in Jerusalem (Vespasian diverted it to the temple of Jupiter Capitolinus), and had permission to assemble for meals, both ritual and social. They were served by over a dozen different synagogues.

The Greek-speaking Jews of the diaspora always had a sense of exile from their land of origin. They maintained links with Jerusalem, paying their half-shekel Temple tax and making the annual pilgrimage when possible. Yet the religion of the diaspora was not dependent on the Temple. Great cities like Babylon and Alexandria had their schools where the Mosaic Law was studied and taught, schools which came to eclipse those in the Temple courts. When the Temple was destroyed in AD 70, it was rabbis like Yohanan ben Zakkai who showed the way ahead.

> When a disciple of Yohanan ben Zakkai wept at seeing the Temple mount in ruins, Yohanan asked him, 'Why do you weep, my son?'
>
> 'This place, where the sins of Israel were atoned, is in ruins, and should I not weep?' the disciple replied.
>
> 'Let it not be grievous in your eyes, my son,' Yohanan replied. 'For we have another means of atonement, as effective as Temple sacrifice. It is deeds of loving kindness, as it is said (Hosea 6:6), "For I desire mercy and not sacrifice."'

The Roman Prefect – Pontius Pilate

The outlying provinces of the Roman empire, those run by the Roman army, came under the direct authority of the emperor at Rome. To each province he appointed a deputy known as a legate, usually a wealthy man from a family of senatorial rank.

Under the Roman system young aristocrats were able to start near the top, without working their way up through subordinate ranks.

The territory of Pontius Pilate, as he is called in the Gospels, was Judaea and Samaria, which formed part of the Roman province of Syria. At the time the legate for Syria had his headquarters in Damascus. Pilate held the lower rank of prefect (the title was changed to procurator in AD 41). He reported immediately to the legate and ultimately to the emperor in Rome. Pilate's own headquarters was the coastal town of Caesarea, built by Herod the Great in honour of Caesar Augustus. A stone found there bears the inscription:

Pontius Pilatus Praefectus Provinciae Judaea.

We know the Roman *praefectus* by these his second and third names; his first name, the one by which he would be called in his own household, is not recorded. As a complete guess, made in order to break up the over-familiar pattern of his name, I suggest that it might have been Gaius. Pontius suggests *pons*, a bridge, while Pilatus probably originally meant one armed with a *pilum*, the legionary javelin. Born into the equestrian class of Rome, Pilate would have served in the army and in a middle-ranking to senior command. We may surmise that whatever Pilate had learnt about leadership had been acquired in the camp and campaigns of the Roman army.

The backbone of the Roman army was the centurions of the legions. They were a tough breed of men, cast in the Spartan mould. Some of them proved to be too harsh and overbearing. In a mutiny that broke out after the death of Caesar Augustus in AD 14, the soldiers lynched one centurion whom they had nicknamed *Cedo Alteram* or 'Give-me-Another,' so called because when he had broken his vinewood cane of office on a soldier's back he did not rest but demanded another stick and another. Acting like both a modern company commander and a sergeant-major in one, most centurions, however, were natural leaders. They had risen through the ranks and they had learnt their business the hard way. They led from the front.

As a young officer aspiring to be a good leader of the Roman legionaries, whose example might Gaius Pontius Pilatus seek to emulate? Perhaps one of them might have been Gaius Marius, who had been responsible for a major reorganization of the Roman army over a hundred years earlier. Like himself Marius came from a family of equestrian rank. As a young man, he had served on the staff of a Roman army then campaigning in North Africa. Although lacking in wealth and eloquence, he had an unusual confidence in himself, coupled with a great capacity for hard work. In writing about Marius in this period of his life, Plutarch made some comments about Roman soldiers which are both illuminating and generally applicable in leadership well beyond the military sphere.

> It was a hard war, but Marius was not afraid of any under-taking, however great, and was not too proud to accept any tasks, however small. The advice he gave and his foresight into what was needed marked him out among the officers of his own rank, and he won the affection of the soldiers by showing that he could live as hard as they did and endure as much. Indeed it seems generally to be the case that our labours are eased when someone goes out of his way to share them with us; it has the effect of making the labour not seem forced. And what a Roman soldier likes most is to see his general eating his ration of bread with the rest, or sleeping on an ordinary bed, or joining in the work of digging a trench or raising a palisade. The commanders whom they admire are not so much those who distribute honours and riches as those who take a share in their hardships and dangers; they have more affection for those who are willing to join in their work than for those who indulge them in allowing them to be idle.

Much later Marius did get himself elected consul seven times, the first Roman in history to do so. But he was no political leader. In the Senate, when his victories had already brought him a huge reputation, Marius used to behave quite timidly if hecklers attacked him. All the steadfastness and firmness which he showed in battle seemed to drain from him when he stood up to speak in popular assembly, so that he could not cope with even the most ordinary compliments or criticisms. Clearly his style of military command was not transferable to the world of politics, where citizens look up to someone essentially equal for leadership that respects their freedom and dignity. Marius lived to be seventy, his harsh nature turning savage and vindictive by the possession of supreme power. He gave the Romans their first real taste of tyranny.

On a much smaller stage Pontius Pilatus, too, faced the challenge of moving from a position of military command to exercising headship in a civil field as a Roman governor. How would he fare?

A more recent and much greater example of Roman leadership was Julius Caesar. Pilate's grandfather would have been young enough to have served under Caesar. If so, perhaps he told his grandson some of his memories of Caesar in the field. Caesar's very presence seemed to transform the professional Roman legionaries into men of extraordinary valour. 'Soldiers who in other campaigns had not shown themselves to be say better than average,' wrote Plutarch, 'became irresistible and invincible and ready to confront any danger, once it was a question of fighting for Caesar's honour and glory.' Plutarch cited examples, such as this one:

> There was the occasion in Britain when some of the leading centurions had got themselves into a marshy place with water all round and were being set upon by the enemy. An ordinary soldier, while Caesar himself was watching the fighting, rushed into the thick of it and, after showing the utmost daring and gallantry, drove the natives off and rescued the centurions. Finally, with great difficulty, he made his own way back after all the rest, plunged into the muddy stream, and, without his shield, sometimes swimming and sometimes wading, just managed to get across. Caesar and those with him were full of admiration for the man and shouted out to him in joy as they came to meet him; but the soldier was thoroughly dejected and, with tears in his eyes, fell at Caesar's feet, and asked to be forgiven for having let go of his shield.

Apart from his open-handed generosity with the rewards of victory – a trait which King David and Alexander the Great shared – Caesar led by example. There was no danger which he was not willing to face, no form of hard work from which he excused himself. Like Alexander the Great, his great exemplar, Caesar had a passion for distinction which enabled him to over-come the disadvantages of a slightly built physique, and a prone-ness to migraine and epileptic fits. 'Yet so far from making his poor health an excuse for living an easy life,' continued Plutarch, 'he used warfare as a tonic for his health. By long hard journeys, simple diet, sleeping night after night in the open, and rough living he fought off his illness and made his body strong enough to stand up to anything.'

The Roman army worked reasonably well operationally with-out inspiring leadership. It was a military machine held together by the ropes of discipline. Compliance with orders was achieved by the exercise of power; whether or not the men were willing was a matter of secondary importance to some commanders and of no importance to others. But the Roman soldier had the same human nature and desire to excel as his Greek counterpart. Greatness was always latent in the legions, awaiting the call to life from a leader of genius. Caesar was such a leader. Under Caesar's eye the Roman legions became 'an unconquered and unconquerable army'.

Caesar's nephew and heir Octavian inherited this legacy of leadership as well as his uncle's family name. He was granted the title of *Augustus* on becoming emperor in 27 BC. The Roman historian Duo Cassius puts into the mouth of Maecenas, one of Augustus Caesar's most trusted advisers, this reminder of the ideal of Roman leadership:

> If you yourself do whatever you would wish someone else who ruled you to do, you will not go wrong. How can all fail to regard you with affection as father and saviour, when they see you are disciplined and principled in your life; good at warfare but a man of peace; when you show no arrogance and do not take advantage; when you meet them on a footing of equality, and do not yourself grow rich while demanding

money from others; are not yourself given to luxury while imposing hardships upon others; refrain from licentiousness while reproving it elsewhere; when, instead, your life in every way is precisely like theirs?

These words express the Roman ideal of leadership – grounded on the foundations of Greek thought and experience – at its most noble. For, harsh, aggressive and grasping as the Romans tended to be, at their best they did have a sense of vocation to provide the nations under their dominion with a wise and just leadership. 'Let it be your task, Roman, to control the nations with your power (these shall be your arts) and to impose the way of peace, to spare the vanquished and subdue the proud!' As these words of Virgil in the *Aeneid* suggest, Rome saw itself as more than a conqueror. By its military might Rome brought peace to a warring world. Law and order, together with the more material benefits of cities and towns, roads and aqueducts, followed in the wake of the victorious legions.

How far did Gaius Pontius Pilatus live up to these ideals as a Roman leader? Quite apart from his civil responsibilities in Judaea and Samaria, he was now in command of about 4000 soldiers, some Roman but mostly cohorts of auxiliary units. The first fact to note is that Pilate served for the relatively long period of ten years (AD 26–36) as *praefectus*, which suggests that on the whole he governed well. His domain was one of the most difficult territories in the Roman empire to rule. Had he been incompetent or bad, the legate in Damascus or the emperor in Rome – who kept his finger on the pulse of events – would not have left him in office for that length of time. He must have had in some measure the Roman virtues of *gravitas* (dutiful and constructive purposiveness), *constantia* (persistent endurance), and *libertas* (love of legal and political rights).

True, Gaius Pontius Pilatus did not begin well upon taking office, most probably because he lacked experience as a governor. Josephus tells us that he offended Jewish sensibilities by allowing the legionary standards with their eagle emblems and images of Caesar – objects of worship – to be brought into Jerusalem. Moreover, understandably from our viewpoint, he used money from the Temple treasury to pay for a much needed aqueduct some twenty-three miles long to bring water to the city. He also broke up a riot by disguising his soldiers and getting them to mingle with the crowd, which looks like a clever stratagem. Luke mentions, too, a mysterious incident – if indeed it was historical – about some Galileans whose blood Pilate 'mixed with their sacrifices'. Perhaps that refers to the same riot. Philo of Alexandria, a contemporary of Pilate's, has nothing but bad to say about him, but he was far from the scene and gives no examples to back up his accusations.

Here I must admit to a certain empathy with Gaius Pontius Pilatus. While serving in the Arab Legion in 1954 I found myself in temporary command of an infantry regiment of 800 legionaries. This Bedouin regiment was the garrison of the walled city of old Jerusalem. The Tower of Phasael, once part of Herod the Great's palace which stood in the upper city, was my headquarters, just as it had been for Pilate. In front of the gates of the Citadel which enclosed the Tower stood our armed Bedouin sentries, their red-and-white *shemaghs* wrapped around their heads. Here had once stood Pilate's judgment seat. For about two months the responsibility for keeping law and order in that volatile city – it was election time – fell on my shoulders. And so I have some idea of how Pilate must have felt. It even fell to my lot one moonlit night to stand in the olive groves near Gethsemane with a hundred legionaries waiting to arrest a trouble-maker and his gang who threatened to disrupt the elections. Pontius Pilatus had no easy task.

In fact it was not trouble in Jerusalem or even Judaea that brought the rule of Gaius Pontius Pilatus to a somewhat unhappy end. Some Samaritans were largely to blame. A trouble-maker in the territory of Samaria had promised to lead a treasure hunt to the top of Mount Gerizim where Moses, so he claimed, had buried gold and silver vessels. A crowd of gullible Samaritans, many of them armed in order to protect their future riches, prepared to follow him. Or so they said. Pilate, sensing a possible armed insurrection, promptly blocked the ascent with some heavily armed troops. The fight that followed became a massacre. To make matters worse, various Samaritans taken alive were summarily put to death. At this, the people of Samaria made a complaint against Pontius Pilatus to the legate of Syria, one Vitellus. He referred the matter to Rome, and Pilate received a summons to explain his conduct in person to the emperor's advisers. However, before Pilate's ship could reach Rome Emperor Tiberius died. What happened to Pilate is unknown – he passes silently out of history.

Today the name of Pontius Pilate lives solely because of the part he played in the trial and execution of Jesus of Galilee. I wonder if Pilate could even recall the face of Jesus in those later and more obscure years of his life? I believe he did. For the quality above all others which Romans admired was courage in the face of certain death, the kind of courage which they saw gladiators display in the arena. Could Pilate have forgotten a man who had stood before him so calmly when his silence – as Pilate had told him – would lead to certain death? Did Jesus at some point lift his gaze and look Pilate in the eye, the look of a man without fear?

The Tetrarch of Galilee – Herod Antipas

It was the grandfather of Herod Antipas, Antipater the Idumaean, who had founded the family fortunes. After Pompey's conquest in 63 BC of the land the Romans called *Palestina* (from the Greek word for Philistine, *Phillista*), Antipater, who served as *strategos* or governor of Idumaea under the Hasmonaeans, rose to power as the ruler of Judaea.

The Idumaeans were descendants of the Edomites, Semitic cousins of the Israelites who inhabited the land east of the Dead Sea. Some of them migrated into southern parts of Judaea during the troubled times when the successors of Alexander the Great in Syria and Egypt fought to control the land. After the Roman conquest, Antipater was made a Roman citizen and then appointed to rule over Judaea. He delegated to his eldest son Phasael the command of Jerusalem. He entrusted the region of Galilee in the north to his second son Herod, a tall young man of about twenty-five.

Herod soon proved himself to be an energetic and capable

military leader, just the kind of ruler the Romans liked. He suppressed a host of brigands that infested the hill-country of Galilee. His action in summarily executing their leader, a certain Hezekias, without a hearing led to Herod being himself brought to trial before the Sanhedrin, but he went into exile to Rome before sentence was given. It was a shrewd move. For in 40 BC Antigonus, the last of the Hasmonaeans, established himself as king in Jerusalem with the help of the Parthians. Now the Parthians were Rome's greatest and most feared enemy in the East, therefore Herod had little difficulty in persuading the Senate in Rome to appoint him as king of Judaea in the place of Antigonus. Not without boldness, Herod then returned to Palestine with a military force and in 30 BC he captured Jerusalem after a siege. It is said that in an orgy of vengeance he had members of the Sanhedrin put to death. With Roman military might behind him, bearing the title of king on the Roman Senate's authority, Herod never wavered in loyalty to Rome during his long reign of thirty-four years. His most unpopular act, that of placing a golden eagle above the Temple gate in honour of the Romans, was symbolic of his debt to them.

Herod the Great was not a popular ruler. Even his prompt provision in time of famine, and a partial remission of taxes, won him no hearts among his Jewish subjects. The Jerusalem aristocrats most probably looked down on him as being low-born and not fully a Jew. Herod was a great builder of cities, palaces and fortresses in the Hellenistic style, as if he were seeking to transform his backward country into a land fit to belong to the Roman empire. He built in or near Jerusalem, for example, massive theatres, a stadium for athletic contests, and a hippodrome for horse and chariot races. An athlete himself in his youth, Herod once attended the Olympic games. In other places he erected temples dedicated to Caesar Augustus. It is ironic that perhaps his most splendid work in the Hellenistic style – the Temple in Jerusalem which he rebuilt – would one day be burnt down by the Romans. The 'master course' of huge stones – one more than 40 feet long and calculated to weigh 370 tons – served to stabilize the entire building and has protected it against several earthquakes over two millennia. It was these 'wonderful stones' that a disciple pointed out to Jesus (Mark 13:1). The 'wonderful buildings' they saw included gleaming white marble buildings, and colonnades and porticoes of marble Corinthian columns around spacious courts. The whole Temple platform occupied one-sixth of the walled city.

As a reward for his loyalty and long service to Rome, Augustus granted Herod the right to dispose of his kingdom to his sons as he wished. By terms of his will, when he died in 4 BC, his son Archelaus was appointed king over Judaea and Samaria, while Archelaus' younger brother Herod (called Antipas by Josephus) was given Peraea and Galilee with the title of *tetrarch* – literally the ruler of a fourth part. He was seventeen years old. The half-brother of the pair, Philip, was given the same title. His fourth share consisted of land to the north-east of Galilee, a large volcanic region strewn with boulders of black basalt for the most part of it. It included areas known as Trachonitis, Gaulanitis, Aurantis, Batanaea, Gaulanitis and Paneas, but their boundaries on the map are hard to determine.

As king of Judaea and Samaria, Archelaus lasted no longer than ten years. When a riot broke out in Jerusalem, his soldiers massacred a large number of people including some pilgrims who happened to be visiting the city for the feast of Passover, the great Jewish spring pastoral festival and celebration of the Exodus. The people of Judaea petitioned Augustus Caesar to remove him as king. Archelaus was reduced in rank to *ethnarch*, leader of the people, but it did not teach him a lesson. After many acts of tyranny and violence, he was finally banished by Augustus to Gaul. In his place the Romans appointed a *praefectus* over Judaea and Samaria as part of the Province of Syria.

By contrast Herod Antipas continued to govern Galilee as *tetrarch* over a period of forty-three years. Yet the facts of his life are sparse. Like his father, though on a smaller scale, he remodelled cities, public buildings and fortresses in the Hellenistic style. For example, he rebuilt and strongly fortified Sepphoris in Peraea, and Betharamatha for the protection of Galilee. In AD 22 he also built a new capital, Tiberias, named in honour of Emperor Tiberius, on the western shore of the Sea of Galilee, which was henceforth known as the Sea of Tiberias. The new capital was governed like a Greek city with a council of 600 members, an *archon* and all the other officials.

Meanwhile, Antipas' neighbour Philip rebuilt Paneas at the foot of Mount Hermon and called it Caesarea Philippi in honour of Augustus, adding his own name, perhaps a little egotistically, to avoid confusion with the city on the Mediterranean coast. He also rebuilt Bethsaida on the Sea of Galilee, calling it Julias after the daughter of Augustus before she fell from favour. Philip married Salome, daughter of Herodias by her first husband, notorious to us for her reputed part in the death of John the Baptizer. After an uneventful and peaceful reign he died in 33 or 34, being the twentieth year of the reign of Tiberius.

On a visit to Rome, Herod Antipas had met this same Herodias. She was the daughter of Aristobus, a son of Herod the Great and Mariamme, daughter of a Hasmonaean high priest. Perhaps Antipas hoped that marrying her would win him the support of the Sadducees. She was a sister to Herod Agrippa I of Judaea and Samaria. Antipas was her half-uncle. She agreed to leave her present husband (another of her half-uncles) for him if Antipas would divorce his wife. This Antipas did, but at the cost of a war with her father Aretas, King of the Nabateans, whose capital lay in the mountain-girt city of Petra. The war petered out in ignominious defeat for Herod and his army. This second marriage of Herodias was especially offensive to the stricter Jews, because her first husband and father to her daughter was still alive.

When Herodias' younger brother Herod Agrippa, who had been living in Rome, had to flee from his debtors she prevailed on Antipas to give him refuge. This grandson of Herod the Great had assumed the name 'Agrippa' on account of a friendship with Marcus Vipsanius Agrippa, son-in-law of Emperor Augustus. Antipas gave him a house in Tiberias and an income as inspector of its market. Whether Agrippa ever set eyes on Jesus, who lived in Galilee at the time, we do not know. Eventually Agrippa quarrelled with Antipas at a feast in Tyre where both men drank too much. Agrippa departed to make his complaints about Antipas to the legate of Syria, but he received no encouragement there either – and so made his way back to Rome where he resumed his former spendthrift life. By a stroke of luck, however, Agrippa became a great favourite of Gaius, the man destined to succeed Tiberias as the Emperor Caligula in AD 37. Caligula loaded his friend Agrippa with honours and gifts, including the tetrarchy of his uncle Philip after his death and other northern territories with, eventually, the title of king. The Senate made him an honorary *praetor* and subsequently advanced him to consular rank.

Stirred by envy at the advancement of her brother Agrippa to full royal dignity, Herodias persuaded her husband to travel to Rome to seek from Caligula the title of king. When Antipas reached Rome, however, he found Agrippa already there and spreading poison about him. Resurrecting a charge he had first made to Tiberius, Agrippa accused his brother-in-law of the worst crime of all: plotting with the Parthians and amassing military supplies for some 70,000 soldiers in order to overthrow Roman rule. It appears that Herod Antipas did not offer any defence, which was tantamount to pleading guilty. Pontius Pilatus was almost certainly in Rome at the time, and doubtless his opinion would have been sought. Eventually Caligula sentenced Herod Antipas to lifelong exile in Gaul. Herodias refused the emperor's chivalrous offer to exempt her from exile – probably because she was Agrippa's sister. Displaying a flash of the old Hasmonaean spirit, and perhaps a love for her husband, she chose to accompany him to Gaul. The tetrarchy of Herod Antipas and all his other property were given by Caligula to the instrument of his downfall – the ungrateful and disloyal Agrippa.

Agrippa reigned, as King Herod Agrippa I, for three years, much approved at first by the Pharisees. He persecuted some who belonged to the church (Acts 12). He killed James the brother of John with the sword and imprisoned Peter, though the latter made a miraculous escape. Agrippa had the defaulting sentries put to death. One day Agrippa ascended his throne in a silk robe woven with silver that shimmered in the light in order to receive a deputation from Tyre and Sidon suing for peace. After his oration to the ambassadors the obsequious courtiers around him cried out, 'The voice of a god, and not of man!' They fell on their faces and worshipped him. Shortly afterwards Agrippa died of a sudden heart attack or stroke. The Jews rejoiced at his death, seeing it as a divine act of punishment for his blasphemy. In distant Gaul, when the news of Agrippa's fate and subsequent obloquy reached them, Herod Antipas and Herodias must have smiled across the table at each other.

As the story of his deception of Rome suggests, Herod Antipas was a master of the art of dissimulation. He must have been as much an enigma to the Romans as to his countrymen. What Pontius Pilatus thought of him we do not know, but Luke's Gospel mentions that a hostility existed between the two men. According to the same source, that enmity was somehow ended by the action of Pilate in sending Jesus as a prisoner to Antipas and the manner in which he returned him to the Prefect for sentence (Luke 23:6–12).

It seems that Pilate, hearing that Jesus was a Galilean and 'belonged to Herod's jurisdiction', sent him across the city to the house of Herod Antipas, presumably for judgment. But under Roman law crimes were punished under the jurisdiction of where they were committed (*forum delicti*), and no charge worthy of capital punishment was brought against Jesus for anything he had done in Galilee. It is just possible that Pilate had heard that Herod Antipas regarded Jesus as a prophet, perhaps John the Baptizer brought to life again. Such a prophet and miracle-worker might serve Antipas' own seditious purpose against the Romans. Pilate was not without his spies and informers, and he may have suspected Antipas. If so, it was a cruel thrust on Pilate's part as if to say, 'Here is your prophet, what do you think of him now?' Alternatively, knowing of Herod's deep desire to set eyes on Jesus, Pilate may simply have seized an opportunity to do Antipas an unsolicited favour, and thereby to put him in his debt.

'When Herod saw Jesus, he was very glad, for he had long desired to see him, because he had heard about him, and he was hoping to see some sign done by him. So he questioned him at some length; but he made no answer.' Whatever truth Jesus had to utter, it was not for Herod's ears. Although Luke next mentions some Jewish accusers, it is doubtful that there was any form of trial before Antipas. No sentence is passed. Herod and his soldiers, it is said, treated Jesus with contempt and mocked him. They dressed him in a fine shimmering robe – perhaps from Herod's own wardrobe – and returned him to the Tower of Phasael. 'Herod and Pilate became friends with each other that very day, for before this they had been at enmity with each other.'

My own interpretation of the story, for what it is worth, is that Pilate sensibly asked Herod Antipas for his opinion on Jesus' guilt, and that Herod Antipas took this request as a compliment. The silence of Jesus under questioning from these men in the chief positions of authority could be taken as a form of dumb insolence. Yet even so, Herod Antipas may have been trying to save Jesus' life. Jesus was not punished with a beating, but mocked, albeit with some brutality, as if he were a harmless pretender. Even that 'gorgeous apparel' can be seen as a message from Antipas to Pilate that Jesus' royal pretensions are not to be taken seriously. It is as if Herod is saying to Pilate, 'Look, this man is no threat – I have given him the appropriate punishment, which is to make him an object of laughter and scorn. He is quite harmless. My advice is to give him a beating and to let him go free.'

If this was his intention, then it was a clever if not cunning stratagem on the part of Herod. In Galilee a year or so earlier Jesus had called him 'that fox' (Luke 13:32), possibly in that context alluding to a fox's reputation for being able to keep an eye on someone without appearing to do so. It is true that to the contemporaries of Jesus, to call a person a 'fox' suggested also one who is an insignificant or base person; one who lacks real power and dignity. Yet it also designated one who uses cunning deceit to achieve his ends. Did the Galilean 'fox' try to cheat the Roman 'eagle' of its prey? I believe he did. It *almost* worked. For Luke continues:

> Pilate then called together the chief priests and the rulers and the people, and said to them, 'You brought me this man as one who was perverting the people; and after examining him before you, behold, I did not find this man guilty of any of your charges against him; neither did Herod, for he sent

him back to us. Behold, nothing deserving death has been done by him; I will therefore chastise him and release him.' (Luke 23:13–16)

Perhaps Herod Antipas deserves to be remembered as the man who *almost* saved the life of Jesus. Perhaps, too, it was an act of penitence, some atonement for his remorse over the unpremeditated sin in killing John the Baptizer. If so, then Herod Antipas was 'not far from the kingdom of God'.

4

The Forgotten Leader –
John the Baptizer

What did you go out into the wilderness to behold? A reed shaken by the wind?

Jesus on John, Matthew 11:7/Luke 7:24

In the fifteenth year of the reign of Tiberius Caesar, about AD 30, many Jews from the territories of Herod Antipas and Philip and from further afield flocked to the banks of the River Jordan to see and hear for themselves something they had only read about in the scriptures – a prophet of God. For in that year, Luke wrote, 'the word of God came to John the son of Zechariah in the wilderness'. It was in another wilderness much further to the south that Moses, while tending sheep, had also heard 'the word of God' and had responded to the call to lead God's people Israel away from the bondage of Egypt.

To the villagers and townsfolk who crowded out to see him, John must have seemed a strange figure. He wore a simple garment of camel's hair – a tunic or possibly a rectangular woven blanket such as the lowest Bedouin would wear as a cloak – and either a leather belt or leather loincloth. He ate 'locusts and wild honey', namely cakes of dried locusts mixed with wild honey and cooked in olive oil, a food of the poorest Bedouin down the ages in their struggle to survive in the barren deserts. According to the *Gospel of Ebionites* these cakes tasted 'like manna', which links the fare of John with the heavenly food that sustained Israel in its desert wanderings under the leadership of Moses.

A New Elijah

For the Jews who saw him, John's appearance in a camel's hair mantle or cloak would instantly recall the image of the prophet Elijah. For the rough cloak of camel's or goat's hair which Elijah had worn was, as it were, his trademark. Indeed, since his day it was customary for all prophets – true or false – to present themselves dressed in the mandatory garb. By presenting himself in this way John provoked the question in the people's minds: is this man not Elijah resurrected in the flesh? If so, it would be a portent of immense significance. The key to its meaning lay in the prophecies of the Bible.

First, who was Elijah? The Book of Kings includes a set of vivid stories and legends about him. Elijah the Tishbite lived in the ninth century BC. As a prophet inspired by God he emerged as the leader in a bitter struggle against the worship of Baal – the principal fertility and agricultural god of the Canaanites. It was the Tyrian princess Jezebel, who had married Ahab king of Israel, who was responsible for the pressure on her husband's subjects to bow down before Baal.

Elijah began his mission to oppose her by prophesying a drought in the land. Led by God, Elijah himself withdrew to the desert east of the River Jordan where he was miraculously fed by ravens. In that wilderness, Elijah dressed in the hairy mantle and leather belt or loincloth. The mantle, which he bequeathed to his successor Elisha, had miraculous properties, like the staff of Moses.

There was a common belief that Elijah would one day reappear to herald the 'day of the Lord', the day when God's rule or kingdom would be established over all the earth (Isaiah 40). Around 450 BC, in the vision of the prophet Malachi (4:5–6), the role of Elijah is specifically mentioned:

Behold, I will send you Elijah the prophet before the great and terrible day of the Lord comes. And he will turn the hearts of fathers to their children and the hearts of children to their fathers, lest I come and smite the land with a curse.

In Hebrew the idea of 'turning', as turning about on a road, lay at the heart of the concept of repentance. The task of Elijah returned in the flesh was clear: to offer Israel one last opportunity to repent before the 'day of the Lord' fell on them like a thunderstorm. For only the truly penitent would stand in that day and find it full of blessing. The wicked or evil, at least those of them who failed to repent, would face a very different fate. For, as Malachi wrote (4:1–3), God's day will come with fire, 'burning like an oven'. The impenitent evil-doers will be consumed by that divine fire, like dry stubble that is burnt in the fields after the harvest. For those who fear God's name, however, there are words of great hope. In the golden dawn of the new age a 'sun of righteousness shall rise, with healing in its wings'. And the righteous will go forth 'leaping like calves from the stall' and 'tread down the wicked'. Such was Malachi's apocalyptic vision, fashioned from metaphors drawn from everyday life in rural Palestine.

'The beginning of the gospel of Jesus Christ, the Son of God.' These are the opening words of Mark's Gospel. They are immediately followed by this prophecy from Isaiah:

> Behold, I send my messenger before thy face,
> who shall prepare thy way;
> the voice of one crying in the wilderness:
> Prepare the way of the Lord,
> make his paths straight.

'John the Baptizer', Mark continues, 'appeared in the wilderness, preaching a baptism of repentance for the forgiveness of sins.' Matthew alone among the Gospels quotes what John actually said: 'Repent, for the kingdom of heaven is at hand.'

Mark sets the story of John the Baptizer – as he calls him – in the context of his much wider and more important story the good news about Jesus who is 'the Christ' (*Chrestos* is the Greek for the Hebrew 'Messiah', 'the anointed one') and 'Son of God'. In *that* story, John plays the opening role of a herald. In the analogy of a Greek play, it is as if John walks alone on to the stage to introduce the principal actor – Jesus. Lest the audience should miss his significance – given the fact that at first he will hardly stand out from the crowd – John points out Jesus and clearly identifies him as the Messiah and Son of God. John shows a true humility before Jesus, accepting that he himself will be totally eclipsed by this new 'sun of righteousness' rising in the eastern sky. John seems destined to be remembered as the 'best man' of the bridegroom. But is that the full story? It is instructive to consider John independently of Jesus and as a remarkable leader in his own right. What kind of leader was he?

John's First Appearance

It is interesting to try to establish where, on the River Jordan, John first began his work of proclamation and baptizing. According to Mark, followed by Matthew, 'all the country of Judaea and the people of Jerusalem' went out to hear John and to be baptized by him, which suggests a location for his activities on the Jordan a few miles north of the Dead Sea. Luke is much less specific: John went into 'all the region about the Jordan'. In John's Gospel (the Authorized Version), the actual place where John first baptized is called *Betharaba*. Recently, archaeologists have restored some early Byzantine churches and baptisteries in the Kingdom of Jordan which seem to confirm this location as being the traditional place where Jesus came to be baptized.

Yet the early Christian scholar Origen stated that he had himself inserted the name Betharaba into the manuscript of John's Gospel that he had before him. Although 'in almost all the manuscripts' Origen found *Bethany* yet he substituted *Betharaba* – mentioned as one of six cities in the wilderness (Joshua 15:6) – because a place of that name was being pointed out on the Jordan's banks in his day – Origen died in AD 254 – as the place where Jesus had been baptized. He had himself looked for it but found no place called Bethany on the Jordan 180 *stadia* (33 kilometres) from Jerusalem where it was said to be. So he accepted on hearsay that the location was Betharaba, though he did not visit it. Scholars now have dropped Betharaba in favour of the name given in the oldest manuscripts: *Bethany across the Jordan*. It may be so called by the author of John's Gospel to distinguish it from 'the village of Mary and Martha' that John names as Bethany near Jerusalem. Where was this other Bethany?

That question can be answered with some certainty. Bethany was in fact the region of *Batanaea* – the ancient Bashan famed in the Bible for its bulls. It formed part of Philip's tetrarchy, and bordered on Gaulanitis (known to us today from the Golan Heights). Beyond it lay Aurantis, the Hauran or territory of the Jebel Druze – a wilderness of dark volcanic rock and stone. Herod the Great had settled 2000 Babylonian Jews there, and from Batanaea he had recruited mounted archers for his army. Later, the Christian church took root there. Batanaea provided several Christian martyrs, and – in more happy times – it sent a bishop to the Council of Nicaea.

In Aramaic the region was called *Bethaniya*. On the earliest maps the Arabic name is *el-Bethaniya* or *el-Batiya*. By this time the name was clinging to a narrow strip of land bordering the Sea of Galilee on its north-eastern shore just to the east of the River Jordan as it flows into the lake. It was to this place that Jesus walked from Galilee to meet John.

The proximity of Bethany to Galilee helps to explain why most if not all of John's disciples known to us by name were Galileans. Andrew, the first to leave John's side to follow Jesus (according to John's Gospel), was from the nearest town of Bethsaida and so was his brother Simon whom he fetched. We are not actually told that Simon was a disciple of John the Baptizer but the fact that he was relatively close to hand suggests that possibility. Philip, whom Jesus called to be his disciple, was also from Bethsaida. Again, Philip's presence in the wider circle of John suggests that he was a supporter of his, if not actually a disciple. Bethsaida, which in Aramaic means 'the house of fishing', lay on the western edge of Bethany on or near the river. As mentioned above, it had been recently renovated in the Hellenistic style by the tetrarch Philip. Yet another Galilean – Nathanael of Cana – was recruited by Philip, again apparently from those who had been drawn to be with John.

The Work of John

Apart from his proclamation of the imminence of the 'kingdom of God' and the urgent need for repentance, John also wrought healing miracles and acted as a rabbi or teacher to a group of disciples around him. Apart from learning from his more intimate teaching, these disciples were able to help him in his work. For John could hardly baptize himself the veritable flash flood of men, women and children that poured out from Galilee and ever further afield to come to him by the banks of the Jordan. John's disciples would doubtless baptize in his name, offering in effect the same baptism as if John had performed it himself. In other words, John had some men to whom he could delegate part of his work. The disciples of John were expected to fast, and he also taught them to pray in a form that could not have been too dissimilar from the prayer that Jesus in turn taught his disciples.

About ten or twelve years after John's death, Paul, on a visit to Ephesus, came upon some disciples of John the Baptizer. The editor of Acts mentions in passing that 'there were about twelve of them in all' (19:7). It is just possible that the idea of grouping disciples in cells of twelve – the symbolic number of the tribes of Israel – may date back to John.

Only the barest outline is given of the teaching of John. Clearly he taught that repentance was a tree, known by its fruit. The restoration of loving relationships in the family of Israel was to be the principal fruit. Old divisions should give way to a new unity. Even penitent *publicani*, the often corrupt tax collectors who collaborated with the 'unclean' Gentiles, and harlots were to be welcomed back into the family of Israel. There should be a new harmony between those who have and those who have not. For the truly penitent, forgiven by God, should overflow with a generosity similar to that which God had shown to them. 'He who has two coats, let him share with him who has none,' declared John, 'and he who has food, let him do likewise' (Luke 3:11). The unmistakable fruit of repentance is this generous love towards one's neighbour in need, sharing with him one's earthly goods.

A balancing principle is to place a bridle on the acquisitive instinct – the desire to accumulate more than is justly deserved – that lies deep within the human heart. That principle tempers John's admonitions to the particular groups who sought his advice. Some tax collectors, for example, who came to be baptized, asked him, 'Teacher, what shall we do?' John replied, 'Collect no more than is appointed you.' Soldiers, probably from the army of Herod Antipas, also asked him, 'And we, what shall we do?' To them John said, 'Rob no one by violence or by false accusation, and be content with your wages' (Luke 3:12–14). These must be taken as examples of the kind of teaching John gave to those intent upon following God's way.

Yet not all the Jews responded to the call of John. One group notable by their absence was the Pharisees. Most probably some Pharisees, conspicuous in their white linen robes, did journey to Bethany but they did not come forward for baptism. Holding aloof in this way was equivalent to declaring John to be a false prophet, and that his message lacked truth. As the Pharisees, together with the scribes as a whole, were the accepted intellectual and spiritual leaders of Israel, this was a major challenge to John's credibility.

John the Baptizer did not wear a prophet's garb for nothing. He counter-attacked by denouncing his opponents. 'But the Pharisees and the lawyers rejected the purpose of God for themselves, not having been baptized by him' (Luke 7:30). In other words, John and possibly his associates began to declare that the scribes and Pharisees were merely condemning themselves to the dire consequences prophesied by Malachi. Thus, by the banks of the River Jordan in Bethany, the seeds were sown of a long and bitter war of words, polemics (from the Greek *polemos*, war) which before long would lead to bloodshed and persecution.

'You brood of vipers! Who warned you to flee from the wrath to come?' In Luke's Gospel, these words of John are addressed to the 'multitudes that came out to be baptized by him'. Here they are a fire-and-brimstone introduction to the core appeal: 'Bear fruits that befit repentance' (Luke 3:7–8). In Matthew's version, however, John utters these same words 'when he saw many of the Pharisees and Sadducees coming for baptism' (Matthew 3:7). It is most unlikely that the Pharisees, still less the Sadducees, did in fact come in any numbers for baptism. But the harsh denunciation may well suggest the origins of a mutual hostility which was all too evident in the author's own day later in the century.

Why did the 'scribes and Pharisees' as a whole refuse to be baptized? They may have reasoned to themselves that if the 'kingdom of God' did suddenly come, as John was prophesying, they would naturally enter it first. Not only were they 'sons of Abraham', but they also understood and kept the Law of Moses – unlike sinners, tax collectors and prostitutes. It is here that John struck a new and radical note, though not one alien to the prophetic tradition. Whether to the crowds as a whole or to the scribes and Pharisees he continued his 'brood of vipers' speech thus:

> Do not begin to say to yourselves, 'We have Abraham as our father'; for I tell you, God is able from these stones to raise up children to Abraham. Even now the axe is laid to the root of the trees; every tree therefore that does not bear good fruit is cut down and thrown into the fire. (Luke 3:8–9)

In Aramaic the words for *children* and *stones* are very similar, which helped John to make his point in a striking and memorable way. The only criterion for entering 'the kingdom of God', John said, is the universal one of goodness. It is the bearing of good fruit – the fruit of good deeds – in one's life that alone matters. Nothing else counts, not even the much vaunted direct descent from Abraham. The great prophets may have said much the same, but now the message was uttered again in a fresh and uncompromising way to large crowds by an influential and popular preacher. The scribes and Pharisees may well have interpreted John's message as a threat, if not an attack upon some of the fundamentals of their religion.

In the Hands of Herod

According to the Synoptic Gospels, Herod Antipas arrested and imprisoned John for denouncing his marriage to Herodias, an echo perhaps of Elijah's condemnation of King Ahab's wife Jezebel. John is also said to have criticized Herod 'for all the evil things' he had done. And, in a most elaborate and colourful story, Herodias took her revenge. She engineered his execution by a mixture of trickery and clever timing – choosing the moment when Herod was probably drunk at a feast held in honour of his birthday. Yet Herod Antipas, unlike his father Herod the Great or half-brother Archelaus, is not known to have done 'evil things'. Mark's story appears to be a piece of fiction. The historian Josephus suggested a different motive. Herod Antipas, he wrote, 'feared John's hold upon the people whom he greatly incited to the point of sedition'. Presumably, on this reading, Antipas thought it wise to make a pre-emptive strike before things got out of hand. He had John arrested and imprisoned in his fortress of Macchaerus, which lay in his other territory of Peraea to the east of the Dead Sea. From it John would never emerge alive.

What actually happened inside the fortress-palace of Macchaerus? Why did Antipas not have John put to death immediately? Mark records that, in spite of Herodias' grudge against John and her desire to kill him, Antipas would not agree to her pleas for his execution. 'For Herod feared John, knowing that he was a righteous and holy man, and kept him safe. When he heard him, he was much perplexed; and yet he heard him gladly' (Mark 6:20). Matthew (14:5) gave a different reason for the delay in John's execution: Herod wanted to put John to death, but he feared the people 'because they held him to be a prophet'.

There is another possibility. Herod may have taken John into protective custody. As an analogy, during the Reformation the Elector of Saxony spirited away Martin Luther to a remote castle of his called the Wartburg. He did so in order to preserve Luther from his enemies. Assuming for a moment that Herod Antipas was indeed planning to raise a large army and invite the Parthians to support him against the Romans, he might well have looked upon a popular prophet like John as a potential ally. It is interesting that Herod kept John under a fairly loose form of imprisonment, which is odd for one suspected of sedition or even of slandering his wife. John's disciples not only were with him but took messages to and from Jesus and perhaps other leaders of the movement that he had inaugurated. Moreover, Herod Antipas himself talked on more than one occasion with John and, it is said, was much impressed by him. No ordinary prisoner.

It is possible that word from Maccaerus reached the outside world that John the Baptizer actually dined with Herod Antipas, thereby having table-fellowship with him. The apocryphal *Gospel of Barnabas*, which draws on an early Aramaic source (see Note 2), may have an echo of the criticism of those who murmured against John for doing so. It includes this saying of Jesus: 'By the living God, you did not sin, John, in eating with Herod, for it was God's will you did so, in order that you might be our teacher and [the teacher] of everyone that fears God.' A second saying of Jesus from the same source makes John's act in eating with Herod an example of humility: 'So do,' said Jesus to his disciples, 'that you may live in the world as John lived in the house of Herod when he ate bread with him, for so shall you be in truth free from all pride.'

Herodias was clearly a highly political and ambitious woman. She may well have sensed that her susceptible husband was coming too much under the influence of John. According to the earliest extant version of Matthew's Gospel in Hebrew (see Note 1), she said to him: 'Jochanan (Hebrew for John) is not worthy to be with you.' With Hasmonaean and Herodian blood in her veins, Herodias needed no lessons in dealing with rivals. Mark's elaborate story of Herodias' plot to kill John may have evolved from a reliable tradition of her growing animosity towards him.

There can be no doubt, however, that the message of John, if taken seriously, did pose a threat to the established order. It could indeed be taken by others as grounds for inciting the people to sedition, in the forms of commotions and passive resistance to authority if not actual armed insurrection. Even men crowding together for any reason was undesirable as far as rulers were concerned. Herod the Great had prohibited people from not only gathering but even walking together in numbers. Why, for example, should people pay taxes if earthy rulers were *soon* to be dethroned and God's 'kingdom' established?

The potential pitfalls of proclaiming that Israel had no king but God had already been illustrated by the story of Judas the Galilean. When Coponius was *praefectus* in Judaea in AD 6, Quirinus the legate of Syria had come to Palestine in person to supervise the taking of a census there. Its purpose, inevitably, was to collect more taxes. A 'very clever rabbi', as Josephus calls him, named Judas the Galilean began to incite the people to resist the census on religious grounds, 'saying that they would be cowards if they submitted to paying taxes, and after serving God alone accepted human masters'. The Galileans were noted for their extraordinary physical courage, and the words of Judas must have stung their pride like angry bees. A revolt broke out, which the Romans suppressed, and Judas was killed (Acts 5:17). At the time Jesus must have been about ten years of age, old enough to understand what his parents or others told him about these events.

Yet with typical Jewish persistence the sons of Judas would not let the matter rest. They regarded 'God alone as leader and master', Josephus wrote, and would accept no human king, especially an alien one. In the East the Roman emperor was commonly called *basileus*, king. From these first sparks, as Josephus narrates, came the great military uprising against Rome in AD 69. It was the main war-party in Jerusalem three years earlier under Eleazar, son of Simon, who first called themselves Zealots. One of these sons of Judas, Menahem, seized the Herodian armoury in the mighty fortress of Masada and returned 'like a king' in triumph to Jerusalem. Later, another Eleazar, son of Jairus, another member of Judas' family, commanded the same fortress when it held out defiantly at the end of the revolt against the besieging Roman army.

From this brief history you can see that in the days of John the Baptizer and Jesus, the skies of Galilee were never free from the storm-clouds of violence. Bands of men, potential partisans or bandits, still lived in the mountain caves that Herod the Great had cleared with much difficulty a generation earlier. For example, one of Judas the Galilean's sons, yet another Eleazar, led a large and active band of partisans in Galilee. Felix, the Roman governor, finally captured Eleazar and his captains in AD 52 and sent them to Rome to be paraded as prisoners before execution. 'The bandits whom he crucified,' added Josephus, 'and the local inhabitants in league with them whom he caught and punished, were too many to count.'

Following the line of Josephus, it may well be that Herod Antipas' spies had informed him that some of those caught up in John's movement – if not John himself – were capable of igniting or fuelling this endemic tendency to insurrection. There may be some link here with the cryptic saying attributed to Jesus: 'From the days of John the Baptist until now the kingdom of heaven has suffered violence (or "has been coming violently"), and men of violence take it by force' (Matthew 11:12).

The Aftermath

On the news that John had been executed and that his disciples had taken his body out of the fortress for burial in a tomb, Jesus returned to Galilee. Embarking with a few disciples in a boat, he crossed over into Bethany. All four Gospels say that a large crowd followed Jesus by the land route into Bethany. This suggests to me that many supporters of John now looked to him for leadership in the vacuum created by their prophet's death. Moreover, it was near to the Passover, a time when Jewish nationalistic feelings tended to be on edge.

In Judaea to the south Pontius Pilate would have moved up to Jerusalem from Caesarea, a precaution taken by all Roman governors at Passover time. He would have posted a strong detachment of Roman soldiers in the Tower of Antonia which adjoined the Temple. From its portals the legionaries could sally out along the top of the Temple walls and stand motionless in order to remind the crowds of pilgrims milling about in the courtyards below them of the Roman order. In the days when Cumanus was procurator (AD 48–52) a bored soldier caused a riot by turning around and exposing his backside to the Jews below. The crowd demanded that he be punished for blasphemy. Stones were thrown. Instead of taking the Jews' feelings into account, Cumanus called out more troops. Although they did not attack, the crowds panicked and many were crushed to death in the rush to get away from the Temple.

By the time Jesus went ashore a great crowd had gathered in Bethany, for as he stepped out of the boat 'he saw a great throng'. When he saw the crowd, Jesus 'had compassion on them, because they were like sheep without a shepherd' (Mark 6:34). In other words, they were leaderless. Elsewhere Matthew (9:36) describes the crowds confronting Jesus as 'harassed and helpless, like sheep without a shepherd'. Harassed – the Greek word is literally *torn* – sheep are those whose coats are torn by thorns. Jesus felt their need deeply and he was willing to meet it – the meaning of compassion – but what kind of a leader did *they* want?

The great crowd was said to have been 'about five thousand men, besides women and children'. The men were standing apart from the women and children. When the sun began to set, it is narrated that the men were commanded by Jesus to sit down in companies, 'by hundreds and by fifties'. That implies that they were already standing in these divisions. Almost all armies were divided on the decimal principle into thousands, hundreds, fifties and tens. In practice units varied in size – a Roman century, for example, seldom mustered a hundred men – but that was the principle. It is difficult to avoid the conclusion that this order was a military one.

All four Gospels record the miracle that followed, known to us as the 'Feeding of the Five Thousand'. After the meal, events took a mysterious turn. John's Gospel narrates that Jesus, seeing 'they were about to come and take him by force to make him king', withdrew or fled to the hills by himself. Presumably the disciples had lost Jesus in the commotion. The disciples escaped to their boat, and perhaps hovered offshore into the early hours before giving Jesus up for dead. Then they set out westwards parallel with the shoreline, but soon found themselves rowing hard against a strong headwind. About 'the fourth watch of the night'

– on the Roman system the last quarter of the night or as dawn was breaking – they suddenly caught sight of Jesus walking on the beach. At first they were terrified, saying 'It's a ghost!', and they cried out for fear. But immediately he spoke to them, saying, 'Take heart, it is I; have no fear' (Mark: 6:45–50).

We can only speculate as to what may have happened on that spring day in Bethany. If indeed this great crowd consisted of John's Galilean adherents angry at his summary execution and willing to form themselves into a military force, they looked in vain to Jesus to become their *nasi* or prince. It seems to have been a parting of the ways between him and the now leaderless flock of John. Jesus would create a flock of his own with the help of these few fearful but loyal disciples.

In Retrospect

'What did you go out into the wilderness to behold?' Jesus asks the crowds, speaking of John the Baptizer. 'A reed shaken by the wind? What then did you go out to see? A man clothed in soft raiment? Behold, those who are gorgeously apparelled and live in luxury are in king's courts. What then did you go out to see? A prophet? Yes, I tell you, and *more than a prophet*' (Luke 7:24–6, my italics). The respect and admiration of Jesus for John shines out in these words. One gets the impression that Jesus would not hear a bad word said about him. Whether or not John acted as a mentor to Jesus he was certainly a great example as a self-sacrificial leader. Hence the significance of John as a leader in the context of this book.

John the Baptizer first appeared in Bethany from the wilderness with nothing except 'the word of God'. That word proved to be creative. For it was as if he transformed the stones into people. It was not his destiny to see the 'kingdom of God'. Like Moses he would die without entering into this new Promised Land that he had been called to proclaim. Yet another Joshua was at hand to lead this new people on the next stage of their journey.

Part Two

What Kind of Leader Was Jesus?

5

The Journey of Jesus

Jesus also told them a parable: 'Can a blind man lead a blind man? Will they not both fall into a pit?'

(Luke 6:39)

The Anglo-Saxon root of the words *lead*, *leader* and *leadership* means a path or road. It comes from the verb *leaden*, to travel or to go. The Anglo-Saxons extended it to cover the journeys that people make upon such paths or roads. Being seafarers they used it also for the course of a ship at sea. And, as I have said above, leadership is essentially a journey word too. A leader is the person who, in one form or other, shows the way on that common journey.

On land a leader often shows the way by going before, like a shepherd leading his flock of sheep. On sea a leader on board ship was the helmsman at the steering oar. For in those days a captain of sailors on board ship would be not only the navigator, but also the helmsman, the same man performing all three functions. Later, Paul identified *leaders* (Greek *kybernetes*, steersman, captain, pilot) as one of the gifts of the Spirit to the church in his first letter to the Corinthians (12:28). The word is sometimes wrongly translated as 'administrators', but in fact it clearly means leaders. Incidentally, our English word *governor* (from Latin *gubernare*, to steer) has precisely the same meaning. Governors and governments are called to be leaders.

The story of Paul as a leader is one of a great journey covering some 10,000 miles which starts on the road to Damascus and ends in Rome. It included voyages by sea which gave him a first-hand appreciation of the professional and leadership skills called for in a good *kybernetes*. But, returning to dry land, we have already encountered three great leadership journeys in this book: Moses and the Exodus from Egypt to the Promised Land;

Xenophon and his epic 800-mile march from Babylon to the shores of the Black Sea; and Alexander the Great's legendary campaign of conquest and exploration that took him from Macedon to the very frontier of India. Later examples can be added to the list, such as the *Hegira* (Arabic *hijrah*, flight) of the prophet Muhammad from Mecca to Medina in AD 622, or the Long March of 6000 miles from south-east to north-west China that Mao Tse-tung led his Communists upon in 1934–5 to escape the harassment of Chiang Kai-shek's nationalist forces.

The Vocation of Jesus

Jesus also made a great journey even though geographically it was confined to a much narrower compass than these epics. The starting point was his solemn immersion by John the Baptizer in the River Jordan. From the Synoptic accounts (John's Gospel does not record the baptism of Jesus), it appears that the baptism and Jesus' experience of his vocation went hand in hand. As Jesus emerged from the water (and, Luke added, while he was at prayer), he heard the call of God. The Hebrew phrase *bath qol* is expressive: it means literally 'daughter of a voice'. What did the heavenly voice – or whisper – call him to do? We are not actually told. In the Synoptic Gospels the voice that comes as if from an opening in the clouds is made to testify to Jesus' 'Christian' identity as Messiah and Son of God, but we are left in the dark as to the mission for which God called him. We are told that the 'Spirit of God' descended upon Jesus and entered into him, just as it had done upon the charismatic leaders of Israel after the days of Joshua known as the 'Judges' and upon the line of prophets from Moses to John the Baptizer. But for what work did Jesus receive the Spirit in such overflowing abundance? What journey into the unknown was God calling him to undertake with perfect trust?

The context suggests a clue. The vocation or calling of Jesus has to be directly related to the work that John the Baptizer had initiated. At any rate, the first steps on the journey will have been a call to work alongside John in proclaiming the same message. It is doubtful if Jesus was ever a disciple of John's –

he was too independent of mind – but he must have conversed much with John and those around him. Jesus also withdrew into the wilderness, probably in the barren region beyond Bethany, to prepare himself mentally, spiritually and physically for what lay ahead. After emerging from this seclusion, Jesus and his disciples went into Judaea and it was here that they heard the news of John's imprisonment by Herod Antipas.

The Mission in Galilee

Mark's Gospel (1:14) follows the account of Jesus' sojourn in the desert with these words: 'Now after John was arrested, Jesus came into Galilee preaching the gospel of God, and saying, "The time is fulfilled, and the kingdom of God is at hand; repent, and believe in the gospel."' This, then is the 'good news' of Jesus – 'gospel' is merely the old Anglo-Saxon word for a good tale.

From this account it looks as if Jesus decided at once to step into the vacuum created in Galilee by the removal of John from the scene, so that his work would seamlessly follow on. Herod Antipas could silence John, but not the voice of God.

As narrated in the last chapter, after the execution of John the Baptizer in Macchaerus, there seems to have been a parting of the ways in Bethany between Jesus and the remnant of John's adherents in Galilee. After the confused and unclear events of the episode now usually called the 'Feeding of the Five Thousand', Jesus became the leader of what was in effect a splinter group from John's movement. Its most distinguishing characteristic was loyalty to John's vision of the 'kingdom of God' as a *spiritual* reality. In other words, it was a state of affairs that would be established by God on earth, either directly or with some help from his chosen agent, but not with the aid of violence or force of arms. As we have seen, that volcanic tendency to reach for the sword was never far below the surface in Israel, which made the Jews such a difficult and dangerous people for the Romans to govern.

The manifesto of the 'kingdom of God' which Jesus announced had nothing to do with an armed struggle against the

Romans to re-establish Jewish autonomy and complete religious freedom. If Luke's account (4:16–22) can be accepted, Jesus used the words of the prophet Isaiah to articulate his own vocation and mission:

> And he came to Nazareth, where he had been brought up; and he went to the synagogue, as his custom was, on the sabbath day. And he stood up to read; and there was given to him the book of the prophet Isaiah. He opened the book and found the place where it was written,
>
>> 'The Spirit of the Lord is upon me,
>> because he has anointed me to preach good news to the poor.
>> He has sent me to proclaim release to the captives
>> and recovering of sight to the blind,
>> to set at liberty those who are oppressed,
>> to proclaim the acceptable year of the Lord.'
>
> And he closed the book, and gave it back to the attendant, and sat down; and the eyes of all in the synagogue were fixed on him. And he began to say to them, 'Today this scripture has been fulfilled in your hearing.' And all spoke well of him, and wondered at the gracious words which proceeded out of his mouth.

Jesus was remarkably consistent and persistent in serving these aims. He had that strong sense of purpose which characterizes great leaders and makes them restless if they are not about their business. There is always another mountain to climb, and the appeal of others to pause and enjoy today's successes usually falls on deaf ears. In the following story we can almost feel the energy and determination of Jesus. Having lain down to sleep after a long and full day of work teaching and healing all manner of sick people in Capernaum, Jesus could not rest for long:

> And in the morning, a great while before day, he rose and went out to a lonely place, and there he prayed. And Simon

and those who were with him pursued him, and they found him and said to him, 'Every one is searching for you.' And he said to them, 'Let us go on to the next towns, that I may preach there also; for that is why I came out.' And he went throughout all Galilee, preaching in their synagogues and casting out demons. (Mark 1:35–9)

In the coming months, perhaps for as long as two or three years, Jesus traversed Galilee and its environs on foot proclaiming the 'good news', teaching and healing. According to Josephus, the general who commanded the Galilean forces in the Jewish Revolt, there were over 200 towns and villages in Galilee – he fortified and garrisoned 19 of them. If every village and town were to hear the news Jesus had a formidable task before him. Moreover, he walked as far as the territories of the Syro-Phoenician cities of Tyre and Sidom on the coast, south of Samaria and Judaea, into the tetrarchy of Philip to the north-east and quite far into the regions of the cities of the Decapolis across the Jordan to the east and Peraea to the south-east. From the pattern of these journeys, it looks as if Jesus had a vision of carrying the message to 'all Syria' (Matthew 4:24), or at least to much of the Roman province of Syria.

Such a task, however, was big for one man. Doubtless after much prayer, Jesus chose twelve of his disciples and followers to share his authority and act as fellow emissaries or heralds to preach the kingdom of God and to heal. Jesus instructed them not to seek or accept any money for their work: 'You received without pay, give without pay' (Matthew 10:7–8).

The reputation of Jesus and his disciples as healers and miracle-workers would normally ensure them a warm welcome – the sick would be brought into the marketplace to await their coming. But what if some surly town or village rejected them, their message and their master? The directions Jesus gave to the Twelve in this respect probably reflected his own practice. If a village or town will not receive you or listen to your words, Jesus told them, 'Go into its streets and say, "Even the dust of your town that clings to our feet, we wipe off against you; nevertheless know this, that the kingdom of God has come near"' (Luke 10:10–11). On the day of judgment, he added with a characteristic hyberbole, Sodom and Gomorrah would be better placed than that town.

But Jesus did not curse the offending town, nor enjoin his disciples to do so. The 'woes' he pronounced fall far short of curses, which are prayers or invocations for harm or injury to come upon another. They are more like expressions of deep regret or sorrow at what the other is bringing on their own head. Capernaum is singled out in this way: it is clear that even the abundance of miracles seen in its streets and marketplace did not convince its townsfolk to accept the 'good news' that Jesus proclaimed. Capernaum had made its own fate: in the day of judgment, it would be 'brought down to Hades'. As for its Galilean neighbours, Chorazin and Bethsaida, declares Jesus, had the pagan cities of Tyre and Sidon witnessed the healings done in those places 'they would have repented long ago, sitting in sackcloth and ashes' (Luke 10:13–15).

'Or do we look for another?'

The fact that towns like Capernaum, Chorazin and Bethsaida, despite both seeing and hearing Jesus and experiencing his gifts as a healer, proved to be unresponsive to his message concerning the 'kingdom of God' calls for explanation. One fairly obvious hypothesis concerns the passage of time. As a tentative assumption, the more months which passed without God dramatically intervening to establish his rule on earth as predicted, the less likely it was that Jesus and his disciples would be accepted as true prophets. Like money in the bank consistently drawn upon, the initial stocks of credibility and enthusiasm would become exhausted. For the Book of Deuteronomy (18:22) has a simple but effective test for identifying a false prophet: 'When a prophet speaks in the name of the Lord, if the word does not come to pass or come true, that is a word which the Lord has not spoken; the prophet has spoken it presumptuously, you need not be afraid of him.'

Although Jesus was too wise to name a specific day or date when the 'kingdom of God' would be established, he made it abundantly clear that the time was very *near*. 'This generation', he said, 'will not pass away before all these things take place' (Mark 13:30). The disciples 'will not have gone through all the towns of Israel, before the Son of Man comes' (Matthew 10:23). Like a thief in the night, the 'kingdom of God' will come suddenly, silently, and when people are least expecting it. Thus an expectation was created, and the passage of time would become more and more testing to the faith of those who had been among the first to believe and hope for the promised salvation.

Jesus told a parable about a farmer who went out to sow seed in a newly ploughed field. Some of the seed he cast out of his basket by hand fell on the path and the birds came and ate it up. Other seed fell on rocky ground, where it did not have much soil, and it sprang up quickly, since it had no depth of soil. And when the sun rose, it was scorched; and since it had no root, it withered away. Other seed fell among thorns, and the thorns grew up and choked it, and it yielded no grain (Mark 4:3–7). The 'seed' which sprang up quickly and then withered away suggests disciples, adherents or supporters who had shown initial enthusiasm and commitment, but – as time passed and the sun of everyday reality continued to rise and set – lost their faith and returned home. John's Gospel indeed records one occasion when 'many of his disciples drew back and no longer went about with him' (6:66).

Eventually the continued delay, as it would be perceived, was bound to raise the fundamental question about Jesus: 'Are you he who is to come, or shall we look for another?' This was the question that John had put to Jesus (Matthew 11:3). Being in prison at the time, under the daily shadow of summary execution, John can be forgiven a certain impatience. It was two of his disciples who carried the key question to Jesus.

In reply, Jesus is said to have pointed to his healing miracles and proclamation: the blind receive their sight and the lame walk, lepers are cleansed and the deaf hear, and the poor have good news preached to them. 'And,' Jesus added, 'blessed is he to takes no offence at me' (Matthew 11:6). But if both the incident and Jesus' words are authentic, it seems that he did not answer John's question. For John himself had performed miracles and preached the good news. There is a certain sting in the tail of John's question – 'shall we look for another?' It is as if John is putting pressure on Jesus to prove that he is indeed the 'Coming One' or else to leave the way open for another.

The person and role of the 'Coming One' or 'the One who is to Come' is extremely vague, but John obviously made a distinction between his own preparatory work as a herald and the function of this person or being. The phrase itself goes back to the prophecies of Malachi (3:1–4) and Daniel (4:23). In Malachi the 'coming one' is described as a messenger: 'But who can endure the day of his coming, and who can stand when he appears?' If he were simply that, John himself might fit the description. But, taken as a whole, the 'Coming One' and its cognates such as Messiah, Son of David, Son of God, and Son of Man, suggest someone supernatural, not unlike the heroes of Greek mythology such as Hercules. Above all, the 'Coming One' is God's agent in actually establishing his new order or rule on earth. Then this 'Coming One' or the 'Holy One of God' was expected to preside over 'the kingdom of God on earth', not unlike a Roman legate of a province who was usually an ex-consul of senior senatorial rank personally chosen by the emperor as his deputy and representative.

The Hour Has Come

According to the prophecies in scripture, there were two differ-ent locations foretold where the 'kingdom of God' would appear: Galilee and Jerusalem. The fact that Jesus lingered so long in Galilee might reflect his belief – and of his disciples – that God would appear there in glory as the 'kingdom' dawned (cf. Matthew 4:15–17). If it was not to be Galilee, then it must be Jerusalem. At some point, however, Jesus came to a decision: he must go to Jerusalem. For it was there, it may be surmised that he thought, he must inaugurate the 'kingdom of God on earth'. My second tentative assumption here is that at this point in the journey Jesus did believe – or know – that he had been chosen as the 'Coming One', the destiny for which he had been born. The decision to go to Jerusalem demanded courage at every level, for it had been prophesied (1 Enoch 90:13–27; 2 Baruch 24–9) that the prelude to the sudden emergence of the 'kingdom of God' would be a period of intense trial and tribulation, culminating in a great battle when the 'powers and principalities' of Hell would be destroyed along with their earthly associates, the wicked or evil and their king, Satan.

Satan, the great misleader of humankind, was as real to Jesus and his contemporaries as Abraham, Moses or David. His name in Hebrew means 'adversary' or 'slanderer'. His other name, the Devil, probably goes back to *Deva*, a god of the nomadic Aryan ancestors of the Medes and Persians. As they settled and adopted other gods, they, so to speak, left *Deva* behind them in the desert. Not only was the wilderness the Devil's habitat, but he exemplified its malevolent hostility to humans. The journey that Jesus makes, both in Galilee and Judaea, is like an opposed march through hostile country. Satan is depicted as leader of the opposition. Satan reigns over the gated city of Hades, has legions of apostate angels or demons at his command, and wages unremitting war against God and his will for the blessedness of humanity. Yet he has not lost his original function of being the tempter (James 2:19), having started his mythical career as one of the 'sons of God' or angels to whom God had delegated the task of informing him about human frailties. In John's Gospel, no lesser demons are mentioned: Jesus and Satan engage as if before a cosmic audience of the two rival sides in single combat, like David and Goliath. It could be represented as a duel to the death.

'And they were on the road, going up to Jerusalem, and Jesus was walking ahead of them; and they were amazed, and those who followed were afraid' (Mark 10:32). The reason for this amazement and fear, according to Mark, was that Jesus had taken the Twelve aside 'on the way' and predicted in some detail what would befall him in Jerusalem in terms of his crucifixion. It seems more probable that Jesus told them that the 'kingdom of God' was about to come in Jerusalem. Like a good leader, too, he may have warned them to be prepared for the expected trials and sufferings, like the agonies of a woman in labour, which would precede its birth. In a saying recorded only in

Tertullian's *De baptismo*, Jesus said: 'No one can attain the kingdom of heaven who has not gone through temptation.'

The news that the end of the long road was at last near turned the minds of some of the disciples to the issue of rewards. In a very human way, the disciples fell to discussing among themselves which of them would be the greatest in the 'kingdom of God'. A great messianic feast was expected on the day when the 'kingdom of God' was established. Abraham, Moses and Elijah would sit down with the company, but what seats would they themselves occupy? To the annoyance of the other ten disciples, James and John approached Jesus and petitioned him for the two chief seats at the high table, the one on his left and the other on his right. As status in those days was visible in where one sat at table, the sons of Zebedee were asking Jesus to acknowledge publicly that they were greater than their companions.

With customary adroitness Jesus sidestepped the issue, declaring that God alone could decide such matters. Certainly he had promised the Twelve, as a reward for their services to the 'kingdom of God', the seats reserved for the chiefs of the twelve tribes of Israel. For Simon, in his direct way, had once said to Jesus on their behalf, 'Lo, we have left everything and followed you. What then shall we have?' And in Matthew's Gospel Jesus replies: 'Truly, I say to you, in the new world, when the Son of Man shall sit on his glorious throne, you who have followed me will also sit on twelve thrones, judging the twelve tribes of Israel' (19:27–8). 'Judging' here should be interpreted as being the 'princes' or paramount tribal leaders.

The road to Jerusalem that Jesus was following took them down the Jordan valley, thereby avoiding Samaria. Jesus and his disciples were accompanied by other Galileans, perhaps several hundred, either his supporters or pilgrims making their way to Jerusalem for Passover. As Jesus was leaving the city of Jericho to begin the long walk up through the hills to Jerusalem with his disciples and 'a great multitude' accompanying him, a blind beggar called Bartimaeus, the son of Timaeus, began to chant 'Jesus, Son of David, have mercy on me!' Jesus heard the call, summoned him and healed him. Bartimaeus then 'followed him on the way' (Mark 10:46–52). Later, 'the Way' was the name first used for the spiritual path marked out by the example and teachings of Jesus (Acts 19:9).

The healing of Bartimaeus, however, is almost the last recorded miracle of Jesus. With the exception of the healing of a man born blind at the Pool of Siloam and the raising of Lazarus – both miracles recorded only in John's Gospel – Jesus would perform no wonders in Jerusalem. Perhaps the more sophisticated citizens of Jerusalem, possibly under the influence of the scribes and Pharisees, lacked that faith which is a necessary condition for the healings which Jesus could perform.

After the weary twelve-mile ascent through the hills of the wilderness of Judaea, the party of Galileans finally came over the broad shoulder of the Mount of Olives and caught sight of the walled City of David on the hilltop below them, the new white limestone and marble of the Temple walls, buildings and porticoes gleaming in the sun. There Jesus mounted an ass, with the garments of some followers forming a makeshift saddle. Amid his excited supporters, Jesus rode down into the Kedron valley and up to the east gate. In front of him some Galileans cast their garments on the road, while others cut leafy branches off the trees – John's Gospel says palm trees – and spread them out before him as well. Suddenly, in Mark's version (11:9–10), the whole crowd of disciples, 'those who went before and those who followed', burst into shouts of praise, crying out, 'Hosanna! Blessed is he who comes in the name of the Lord! Blessed is the kingdom of our father David that is coming! Hosanna in the highest!' Luke, even more dangerously, writes: 'Blessed is the King' (19:38). The cry of *Hosanna* (Hebrew for 'Save, we beseech you') was a direct echo of Psalm 118, and that psalm, although it makes no mention of David, best indicates what must have been in their minds and hearts:

> I thank thee that thou hast answered me
> and hast become my salvation.
> The stone which the builders rejected
> has become the head of the corner.
> This is the Lord's doing;

it is marvellous in our eyes.
This is the day which the Lord has made;
   let us rejoice and be glad in it.
Save us, we beseech thee [*Hosanna*], O Lord!
   O Lord, we beseech three [*Hosanna*] give us success!
                               (Psalm 118:21–5)

Matthew, alone, says that this entry was done 'to fulfil what was spoken by the prophet' (21:4), and he quotes Zechariah 9:9: 'Rejoice greatly, O daughter of Zion! . . . your king comes to you . . . humble and riding on an ass, on a colt the foal of an ass'. Famously Matthew misunderstood the parallelism of Hebrew verse and has Jesus riding on *two* asses! Such was the entry of Jesus into Jerusalem. He had reached the end – almost the end – of his journey, but he still had to accomplish the task now expected of him.

In Jerusalem

Jesus spent his days in Jerusalem 'teaching' in the Temple, presumably discussing the 'kingdom of God' under the shade of its colonnades with what scribes or passers-by were willing to listen. But Jesus did not sleep in the city. Perhaps for his own safety, each evening he withdrew to the Mount of Olives. It is possible that he lodged in one of the houses of his friends in the villages which lay on its eastern side.

In Jerusalem the relations between Jesus and the Temple authorities and its resident scribes became increasingly more acrimonious. If the parable known as 'the Wicked Tenants' can be so interpreted, Jesus may well have expected to be stoned to death in the city which he believed had killed all the prophets, and he certainly came close to that fate on at least one occasion. On another, according to John's Gospel, having been charged with blasphemy, or acting as if he were a god, an attempt was made to arrest him. But he escaped and 'went away again across the Jordan to the place where John at first baptized, and there he remained' (John 10:40).

It appears, then, that even Jerusalem, the city of David, had failed to embrace the 'good news' of the 'kingdom of God'. Now it was too late. The hour was at hand. Jesus shook the dust of its streets from his feet, but with a heavy heart: we are told that he wept over the city that he clearly loved. Matthew concluded a list of Jesus' 'woes' against the scribes and Pharisees with this one over Jerusalem:

> O Jerusalem, Jerusalem, killing the prophets and stoning those who are sent to you! How often would I have gathered your children together as a hen gathers her brood under her wings, and you would not! Behold, your house is forsaken and desolate. For I tell you, you will not see me again, until you say, 'Blessed is he who comes in the name of the Lord.' (Matthew 23:37–9)

Even the Temple itself, the probable scene of this lament, would not survive the disaster which Jerusalem had brought upon itself. For Matthew continued:

> Jesus left the temple and was going away, when his disciples came to point out to him the buildings of the temple. But he answered them, 'You see all these, do you not? Truly, I say to you, there will not be left here one stone upon another, that will not be thrown down.'
>
> As he sat on the Mount of Olives, the disciples came to him privately, saying, 'Tell us, when will this be, and what will be the sign of your coming and of the close of the age?' (Matthew 24:1–3)

More questions, more questions.

According to the Synoptic Gospels, Jesus had already – at least symbolically – prepared the Temple, presumably for the 'day of the Lord', by driving out the traders who bought or sold in its precincts, including the money-changers and the stalls of those who sold pigeons for sacrifice. If Jesus did indeed act in the way described – it is his only recorded act involving a degree of violence, however gentle – then his learned contemporaries would link his action into the prophecies of Zechariah. For the ridding of the Temple of all commerce or monetary dealings was part of the vision of Zechariah (Chapter 14). He envisaged a siege of Jerusalem by 'all the nations', who take and ravage half the city, before God suddenly appears:

> Then the Lord will go forth and fight against those nations as when he fights on a day of battle. On that day his feet shall stand on the Mount of Olives which lies before Jerusalem on the east . . .

As described by Zechariah, God's final and decisive intervention in human history would begin with a volcanic-like reshaping of the local landscape around Jerusalem. The Mount of Olives would be split in two, as if by an enormous underground explosion. The sun would stand still in an eternal day, while living waters flowed out of Jerusalem, half to the eastern sea, half to the western sea. 'And the Lord will become king over all the earth; on that day the Lord will be one and his name one,' declared Zechariah triumphantly. The whole land will be flattened except Jerusalem which will stand secure. The survivors of 'all the nations' will go up year after year to worship the King, the Lord of Hosts, and to keep the festival of booths. If they do not so do, they will be punished by drought. Every pot in Jerusalem and Judah will be sacred to the Lord, so all who sacrifice can come and use them and boil the flesh of the sacrifice in them. The vision concludes: *And there shall no longer be a trader in the house of the Lord of hosts on that day.*

The Mount of Olives, then, is the specific place foretold where the 'kingdom of God' will emerge from the womb of time. Perhaps it was here that Jesus could complete the task for which he 'came out'.

The Last Night of the World

The Mount of Olives is about a mile long. It lies on the east of Jerusalem, separated from it by the valley of the Kedron. It forms part of the high ground on that side of the city. One of its two summits had the old name of *Viri Galilaei*, because the 'men of Galilee' who came as pilgrims to the great feasts in Jerusalem had a traditional camping ground in that area. At such times, for example, the townsfolk of Magdala would set up their booths on the Mount of Olives to sell for sacrificial purposes the white doves that abounded in the nearby rocky wadis that opened out to the Sea of Galilee. The Judaean dove-sellers in the Temple precincts were far from pleased with this competition, and eventually put a stop to it. Groves of gnarled olive trees and vineyards stood on its slopes, while fig trees and date palms stood behind the dry stone walls that lined the few dusty tracks traversing it.

The upper room where Jesus and his disciples met for the 'Last Supper' may well have been somewhere on the eastern side of the Mount of Olives. The significance of this last meal – 'this Passover' – was evident in the opening words of Jesus: 'For I tell you I shall not eat it [other ancient authorities read *never eat it again*] until it is fulfilled in the kingdom of God.' The message that the 'kingdom of God' now lay immediately at hand became even more clear in his next words. 'And he took a cup, and when he had given thanks he said, "Take this, and divide it among yourselves; for I tell you that from now on I shall not drink of the fruit of the vine until the kingdom of God comes"' (Luke 22:14–18).

Then, the meal over, Jesus with his disciples left the upper room and went, 'as was his custom', on to the Mount of Olives, and found his way to Gethsemane, Aramaic for 'garden of the oil press'. When he reached the place, he took Simon, James and John with him and said to them, 'Pray that you may not come into this time of trial, the fiery ordeal of the tribulation.' Then Jesus withdrew from them about a stone's throw, knelt down, and prayed.

Jesus is said to have prayed three times – the Hebrew way of expressing completeness. The prayer was divided into these periods by two visits to the three disciples who had fallen asleep. The energy and intensity of the prayer of Jesus seems to have mounted. He became 'greatly distressed and troubled' (Mark 14:33). Some ancient authorities add: 'and being in agony he prayed more earnestly; and his sweat became like great drops of blood falling upon the ground.' The Greek word translated here as 'agony' mean 'shuddering awe'. Jesus had once said that faith could move mountains. Perhaps he was now praying with all his might for the coming of the 'kingdom of God'. It reads like the agony of a woman striving and sweating in labour.

'*Abba*, Father . . . yet, not what I will, but what you will.' Whether or not Jesus actually said these words – who was there to hear? – they perfectly express his humility. For after some hours it must have become apparent to him that God had not answered his prayer in the way he expected. Yet the trust of Jesus in·God was unbreakable. As Job had once said, 'Though he slays me yet will I trust him' (Job 13:15 AV)

The sudden arrival of a band of armed Temple guards outside Gethsemane with lanterns and torches, guided by Judas Iscariot, is extraordinarily dramatic. According to John's Gospel they were accompanied by a band of soldiers and their officer – the Greek words used suggest 250–500 men and a senior commander. If John had his facts right, and if they were – as is most probable – Roman soldiers, then it would seem that Pontius Pilatus was party to the arrest from the beginning. Be that as it may, the armed men entered the place and in the light of the full moon amid the groves of olive trees they arrested Jesus. Judas knew where to take the soldiers, John's Gospel recorded, because Jesus often met in this particular garden with his disciples. Mark tells us that those disciples now 'all forsook him, and fled' (14:50), yet according to the fourth Gospel they remained at his side.

Jesus stepped forward and asked the leaders of the soldiers: 'For whom are you looking?' They replied: 'Jesus of Nazareth.' Then Jesus said: 'So if you are looking for me, let these men go.' It was the act of a true leader. John's Gospel adds: 'This was to fulfil the word which he had spoken, "Of those whom thou gavest me I lost not one"' (18:9). No shepherd cares to lose a single sheep. Yet Simon went out of his way to get himself arrested. He drew a sword and struck a servant of the high priest, but Jesus intervened at once and commanded him to sheathe his blade. A commotion would have ended with a massacre. Whether by Jesus' intercession or by luck, the disciples evaded arrest. Jesus was led alone towards the dark city and his meeting with the high priest Caiaphas.

After the final trial before Pontius Pilatus in front of his head-quarters in the upper city, Jesus was led back into the fortress. There the garrison soldiers stripped him and put on him a sol-dier's red cloak together with a wreath of thorns they had plaited as a diadem for his head, and a reed was placed in his hand as a sceptre. He was beaten with a stick about the head and spat upon in the face. They also blindfolded him and asked him: 'Prophesy, who is it that struck you?' According to the *Gospel of Peter*, the mockery of Jesus was not yet over. Taken outside the gate he was made to sit on the Roman seat of judgment which stood in the large paved square known as *Gabbatha* in Aramaic or in Greek *Lithostroton* (the Stone Pavement) in front of the *Praetorium*. 'Judge justly, king of Israel,' some petitioned Jesus, kneeling in mock supplication, while others pretended to pay homage by bowing low and crying 'Hail, King of the Jews.' Jesus was then led inside once more where he was scourged with knotted whips to weaken him prior to crucifixion.

Finally, Jesus was taken outside the northern gate towards a deserted limestone quarry near a crossroads known in Aramaic as *Golgotha*, 'place of the skull'. The *cruciarius* on such a day was spared no ignominy. He was required to carry the wooden cross-bar or transom (*patibulum*) to the place of execution; he was goaded thither at spearpoint and scourged along the most frequented streets, so that the populace might profit by so signal an exhibition of the fate of criminals. A board whereon the victim's name and offence were inscribed was carried before him.

When they reached Golgotha, Jesus was crucified between two bandits. A crown of thorns was thrust upon his head and the wooden *titulum* with name and offence nailed above it on the cross, with the inscription in Aramaic, Greek and Latin: KING OF THE JEWS (Mark) or JESUS THE NAZARENE KING OF THE JEWS (John). The Roman centurion in charge of the soldiers detailed for this task would have been the commander of Pilate's *officium* of *beneficiari* (guards or orderlies) and *speculatores* (messengers or scouts). The latter doubled as torturers and executioners – it was the *speculatores* on the staff of Herod Antipas who had beheaded John the Baptizer (Mark 6:27). So they knew their grim business.

Luke 23:39–43 tells how one of the *cruciarii* added to Jesus' torment with a prolonged and abusive scolding on the theme: 'Are you not the Christ? Save yourself and us!' The other man cut him short. 'Have you no respect for God?' he demanded. They both suffered as a consequence of their offences, he told the other *cruciarius*, but Jesus had done nothing wrong. Then he said: 'Jesus, remember me when you come into your kingdom.' And the reply came: 'Truly, I say to you, today you will be with me in Paradise.'

6

Jesus and Teamwork

You have that in your countenance which I would fain call
master.' 'What's that?'
  'Authority.'
William Shakespeare, King Lear

Leadership and team working are closely linked. Leaders tend to
create teams, and teams look for leaders. As the Chinese proverb
says: *The bird carries the wings, but the wings carry the bird.*

One of the most striking points about Jesus is that he built
a team of disciples which was probably quite different in function from the disciples who remained loyal to John the Baptizer
both before and after his death. I say 'built', but to be honest,
I am uncertain how far Jesus chose them. It may be that a small
group of John's disciples was already in existence – led by Simon
Peter – who chose Jesus as their leader. The Gospel sources
provide some evidence for both Jesus calling the disciples to be
his team and a team of disciples calling him to be their leader.
My historian's guess is that what actually happened was a mixture of both – Jesus was chosen by some disciples but he also
called others to work with him.

The sharp focus of the Gospels, concentrating like a modern
camera on Jesus, means that others in the field became indistinct.
With the possible exceptions of Simon Peter and Judas Iscariot,
this blurring is true of Jesus' disciples and followers as a whole.
The general impression of the disciples in the Gospels is that, loyal
as they were to Jesus, they remained ignorant of who he really was,
prone to doubt and fear, and sometimes clumsy or insensitive in
handling situations. They had an unfortunate tendency, too, to
desert Jesus in a crisis. According to Christian theology, their
characters and attitudes were transformed only after Jesus had
been miraculously raised from the dead. Then the disciples – or

the core of them – not only knew that Jesus had been all along 'the Coming One', the Messiah or 'Holy One of God', but as a result of these saving events, they also received in due time the same Spirit of God that had filled Jesus while he was alive.

It is an undeniable fact that the reality of the events and experiences we call collectively the 'resurrection' did make an enormous impact on both disciples and the coteries of Jesus' adherents in the environs of Jerusalem and in Galilee. It was the sufficient cause, the spark that gave rise to Christianity. But, as I suggested in the Introduction, one result is that the events and people in the Gospels are seen bathed in the retrospective light of that Christian knowledge. Jesus is portrayed as the *incognito* Son of God, both divine and fully human. By inspired hindsight, the life and work of Jesus are presented as leading up to the fulfilment of his predestined task of dying upon the cross for the sins of the world and being raised again from the dead for the salvation of humankind. There is not much of a role there for a team, which is why they are consigned to the shadows as assistants and usually uncomprehending witnesses.

If, however, historically the true focus of Jesus' life and work was to proclaim the 'kingdom of God' and serve its coming soon on earth, then matters look very different. For Jesus was not alone in that vocation. Through the prophecy of the pioneer John the Baptizer, many men and women were standing ready in the marketplace for hire, willing to dedicate their lives to this newly revealed purpose of God. What they lacked was leadership. Especially after John's murder they were indeed 'as sheep without a shepherd'. What these men and women – or at least some of the more discerning ones – sensed in Jesus was the knowledge, character and powers they were seeking in a leader. For his part, practical wisdom would have told Jesus that he could not complete even the task of proclaiming the gospel throughout 'all Syria' without helpers. He needed a team and doubtless he prayed for one. There are indications, too, that he chose men who were accustomed to teamwork.

The fields, orchards, vineyards, gardens and olive groves of Galilee yielded a surplus of produce that was shipped daily to towns and cities as far afield as Jerusalem in carts pulled by oxen yoked together in pairs. Some of the finest wheat – a luxury as the poor ate barley bread – came from the regions of Capernaum and Chorazin, while Magdala was famed for its linens woven from flax and its 200 varieties of dyed woollen textiles. Olive oil, figs, wine, walnuts, pottery, salted or pickled fish – all these helped to fill the wagons, together with luxury goods. In one parable (Luke 14:15–24), a guest invited to a great feast declined, saying 'I have bought five yoke of oxen, and I am going to try them out; please accept my apologies.' When Elisha received God's call from Elijah it is said that he was ploughing with twelve pairs or yoke of oxen. In fact, the old Anglo-Saxon word *team* meant originally a set of draught animals, such as two or more oxen or horses harnessed together in order to draw a plough or wagon.

Notice that – like *lead* – by origin *team* is associated with journeys: it is a group of animals harnessed together and driven by a teamster to the end of moving or transporting something heavy from one point to another. In early English use, *team* could be used to describe a flock of wild duck or other birds flying in a formation, or to wooden warships sailing in a line of blockade. Figuratively it came to be applied to any instance of persons drawing together, such as in a tug o'war team, or to a definite number of persons forming a side in a match. Thus a team means a number of people associated in some joint activity or work.

In early usage *team* was something applied to a family or brood. Oxen harnessed to plough or wagon pulled better together if they were related. Even today the old image of husband and wife as 'yoke-fellows' is sometimes still used. Two of the pairs of fishermen Jesus called were brothers as well as yoke-fellows. Thomas and Nathanael (of Cana) appear also to have been fishermen, at least occasionally. And it is significant that Jesus sent out his disciples 'two by two', like oxen yoked together.

Fishing on the Sea of Galilee did in fact call from teamwork between boats as well as within boats. As today, there were probably about 250 boats on the Lake (Josephus a little later mentions 330), all that the fish stocks can sustain. The boats were too large for one person to work them alone. Shooting and hauling the trawling net, which was used mainly at night, without a powered winch called for more than one pair of strong arms. In the daytime, when the drag-net was used, the Galilean fishing boats had to work together as a team. The *seine* or drag-net was a large net with weights on one edge and floats on the other used vertically like a wall to enclose fish in a vast space. Then the two extremities were brought together and the whole with its contents dragged ashore. It was easier to work if a great shoal of fish could be netted in the shallows close to the beach. A lookout on the high ground above the most likely bays could help in this respect. His job was to signal to the boats out on the lake when a shoal of fish appeared like a dark cloud sparkling with silver below the surface in the translucent shallows.

Two of the areas in the Sea of Galilee most rich in fish were *el-Batiha* (Bethany) where the Jordan in-flowed, and in the bay of *et-Tabigha* near Gennesaret, where the shallows were warmed by hot springs. It is just possible that Jesus was brought up as a boy in Gennesaret (see Note 1), and if so he would know well the bay of *et-Tabigha* with its flat shore suitable for mooring or beaching fishing boats. Perhaps as a boy Jesus had acted as a lookout and spotted shoals of fish for a few pence or some free fish from the grateful fishermen. Both the Gospels of Luke and John give us stories of Jesus playing just this part and guiding fishing boats with their seine net to a massive shoal of fish. In Luke, Jesus is said to have done so while sitting in a boat, but John – much more plausibly – has Jesus standing on the shore, presumably on some high ground: Here is his vivid account:

> After this Jesus revealed himself again to the disciples by the Sea of Tiberias; and he revealed himself in this way. Simon Peter, Thomas called the Twin, Nathanael of Cana in Galilee, the sons of Zebedee, and two others of his disciples were together. Simon Peter said to them, 'I am going fishing.' They said to him, 'We will go with you.' They went out and got into the boat; but that night they caught nothing.

Just as day was breaking, Jesus stood on the beach; yet the disciples did not know that it was Jesus. Jesus said to them, 'Children, have you any fish?' They answered him, 'No.' He said to them, 'Cast the net on the right side of the boat, and you will find some.' So they cast it, and now they were not able to haul it in, for the quantity of fish. That disciple whom Jesus loved said to Peter, 'It is the Lord!' When Simon Peter heard that it was the Lord, he put on his clothes, for he was stripped for work, and sprang into the sea. But the other disciples came in the boat, dragging the net full of fish, for they were not far from the land, but about a hundred yards off.

When they got out on land, they saw a charcoal fire there, with fish lying on it, and bread. Jesus said to them, 'Bring some of the fish that you have just caught.' So Simon Peter went aboard and hauled the net ashore, full of large fish, a hundred and fifty-three of them; and although there were so many, the net was not torn. Jesus said to them, 'Come and have breakfast.' Now none of the disciples dared ask him, 'Who are you?' They knew it was the Lord. Jesus came and took the bread and gave it to them, and so with the fish. (John 21:1–13)

If a historical event lies behind this story, as I believe it does, there would have been several boats at work. A large shoal in those days could cover as much as an acre of the surface when the ends of the net were drawn tighter and the fish became visible, and so compact in mass that one could not throw a stone without striking several. Hence more than one boat would be used. To work in the shallows, the fishermen would strip to their loincloths. The whole operation called for teamwork.

According to Mark, as already noted, Jesus called two pairs of brothers who were fishermen (Mark 1:16–20). Walking along the shore of the Sea of Galilee he sees Simon and Andrew casting a net in the sea. 'Follow me and I will make you fish for people.' And immediately, we are told, 'they left their nets and followed him'. And going on a little farther, he saw James and John, sons of Zebedee, who were in their boat mending their nets. On hearing his call, they too immediately left their father and followed him. Just as elsewhere Jesus used the metaphor of the harvest – the 'harvest is great but the labourers are few' – so to these fishermen he used the picture of a great shoal of people waiting to be caught. It was a language they could understand. Drop everything, and seize the opportunity while it is there.

The story of Jesus calling the fishermen away from their nets is designed to illustrate his authority as a prophet. When Samuel called David, he abandoned his ewes even though they were about to lamb. When Elijah called Elisha, he paused only to slaughter the oxen with which he had been ploughing. When Jesus called, the Galilean fishermen left their nets still in the water or half-mended on the boat. The need of the 'kingdom of God' is so pressing and so significant for humankind that it can brook no delay, however good the reason. Indeed all reasons are unacceptable excuses. 'Follow me,' Jesus said to one man. But he said, 'Lord, first let me go and bury my father.' But Jesus replied: 'Follow me, and let the dead bury their own dead; but as for you, go and proclaim the kingdom of God.' Even the Mosaic Law – the Fifth Commandment – must give place to the call of God. Another man said to Jesus, 'I will follow you, Lord; but let me first say farewell to those at my home.' Jesus said to him, 'No on who puts his hand to the plough and looks back is fit for the kingdom of God' (Luke 9:59–62).

The Relation of Jesus and his Disciples

To our modern minds the Synoptic Gospels' account of the call of the disciples – the peremptory command to follow and the instant, unhesitating obedience – suggests a military-like relationship between Jesus and his disciples. One antidote against that false impression is the fact, evident above, that for one reason or other not everyone obeyed the summons of Jesus. In other words, there was a choice: you could say yes or no. 'Follow me' was more of a direct personal question, like 'Marry me', than the kind of order a Roman centurion would issue and expect to be promptly obeyed. In fact Jesus had no sanctions to make people stay with him against their will. As we know, many did not respond to his call, or, if they did so, eventually drifted away. Why did a core of disciples choose to stay with Jesus? A clue lies in this passage:

> After this many of his disciples drew back and no longer went about with him. Jesus said to the Twelve, 'Will you also go away?' Simon Peter answered him, 'Lord, to whom shall we go? You have the words of eternal life; and we have believed, and have come to know, that you are the Holy One of God.'
> (John 6:66–9)

'Eternal life' is synonymous with the 'kingdom of God'. What kept disciples like Simon with Jesus was their belief that he alone had the necessary *knowledge* of all things pertaining to the 'kingdom of God'.

It is important to explore the relationship of Jesus and his disciples because it is often taken as a model of discipleship today. The command-and-obey relation which some read into 'Follow me' often breeds the assumption that blind and unquestioning obedience to Jesus is at the heart of being a disciple. For example, in *The Training of the Twelve* (1871) the Scottish divine Alexander Bruce wrote:

> Peter was deficient also as yet in the military virtue of unquestioning obedience to orders, which is the secret of an army's strength. A general says to one, Go, and he goes; to another, Come, and he comes: he appoints to one *corps* its station here, and to another its station there; and no one ventures to ask why, or to make envious comparisons. There is an absolute surrender of the individual will to the will of the commander; and so far as thoughts of preference are concerned, each man is a machine, having a will, a head, a heart, only for the effective performance of his own appointed task. Peter had not yet attained to this pitch of self-abnegation.

Much on the same lines – he even used the analogy of the military commander – the German theologian Karl Heim wrote a book called *Jesus der Herr* or *Jesus the Lord*. The second edition appeared in Germany in 1935, the year when Adolf Hitler became head of state with the designation of *da Führer*, the Leader. Heim suggested that leadership (*Führerschaft*) had now replaced lordship (derived from the Greek *Kyrios*) in our age as the key category for understanding Jesus. Hitherto, he argued, men had only *ideas* about leadership, but now we know what it is like to give unconditional obedience to the Leader (*Führer*). In this sinful world, Heim continued, we can neither guide our own lives nor have any direct knowledge of God. Therefore we need a Leader whom we can unquestioningly follow. The only choice before us is obedience or rebellion. We are sheep, he is the shepherd. Jesus' aim was simply to get people – even in very small numbers – to leave all and follow him '*accepting unconditionally whatever he commands*' (my italics).

Unfortunately we are deeply and painfully aware of where unconditional obedience to the commands of another – or what we perceive to be his commands – can lead. In the historical context, names like Belsen and Buchenwald come to mind. Wise people – those who are intelligent, experienced and good – never do what they are commanded unless they assent to it. The picture of blind or unquestioning obedience painted above has nothing to do with leadership, except perhaps *mis*leadership.

The account in John's Gospel (1:35–51) of how the disciples came to be with Jesus begins, you recall, when two disciples of John the Baptizer heard their master's comment on 'the Lamb of God' 'and they followed Jesus'. Jesus turned round 'and saw them following, and said to them, "What do you seek?" And they said to him, "Rabbi" (which means Teacher), "where are you staying?" He said to them, "Come and see." ' One of the two was called Andrew. He brought his brother Simon to Jesus. 'Jesus looked at him, and said: "So you are Simon the son of John? You shall be called Cephas" (which means Peter)' – 'rock' in Aramaic and Greek respectively. In Galilee next day Jesus came across Philip and said to him, 'Follow me.' Philip in turn brought to him Nathanael of Cana. As the fourth Gospel implies that the 'beloved disciple', the second of the two disciples who stood with John the Baptizer, was John the son of Zebedee, both the pairs of brothers whom Jesus is said to have called away from their nets were probably already disciples of John. Consequently they were already involved to some degree in the work of proclaiming the 'kingdom of God'.

This Johannine account of how Jesus acquired his disciples suggests to me a much more balanced relationship between Jesus and at least his principal disciples. It was more one of 'yoke-fellows' or partners pulling together in a common cause than a commander–recruit, shepherd–sheep, schoolmaster–infant or master–slave pattern of relations. In other words, the disciples were more equal than the other Gospel accounts indicate. Being free and more or less equal, the disciples would respond far better to an inspiring leader than to someone who tried to dominate them.

For true leaders do not seek to create followers, but partners. It is the condition of a slave to have to obey orders promptly on pain of punishment, however unreasonable they may be. The fourth Gospel best captures the spirit of Jesus: 'No longer do I call you servants for the servant does not know what his master is doing; but I have called you friends, for all I have heard from my Father I have made known to you' (John 15:15). In one of the Synoptic Gospels, too, Jesus called his disciples 'my friends' (Luke 12:4). There is no trace of hierarchy or inequality in the relation of friendship. Arguably, to be a friend stresses freedom more than to be a brother or sister, where there is a tie of 'blood'. 'My friends' suggests the companionship, closeness and camaraderie of those who work together in a common cause. Fishermen who daily hauled nets with their partners would know what he meant. It is because Jesus did *not* seek to make others wholly dependent on him that paradoxically the movement survived his bodily absence.

Leadership only really exists among free and equal people, which is why I have emphasized here the stature of the disciples as being not like sheep but more like fellow-shepherds. Together with Jesus, 'the Lord of the harvest' had called them to be 'workers' in his harvest. Later, Paul reflected the philosophy of Jesus in this respect. Apart from some general references to his 'fellow-workers', no less than thirteen different individuals are called, or addressed as, 'fellow-worker' (Greek *synergos*). Writing to the Corinthians about himself and Apollos, for example,

Paul declared: 'We are fellow workers for God' (1 Corinthians 3:9). Again, the stress of the phrase is not on one person being over another, but upon both as looking towards and labouring together for a common goal. 'Not that we lord it over your faith,' Paul told the Corinthians; 'we work with you for your joy' (2 Corinthians 1:24).

Maintaining the Unity of the Team

It is one thing to create the spirit and practice of teamwork, but it is another to maintain the team in the face of external or internal pressures to disintegrate. The seeds of divisiveness and disunity lie deep in human nature, like the seeds of thorns and tares in the barren soil awaiting the spring rains. The competitive desire for status in a group is one perennial source of disunity. Jesus encountered this fact of humanity on the road to Jerusalem, as we have seen, when that dispute had broken out among the disciples about their relative greatness and James and John had approached him for the most important seats at the expected messianic feast.

In Matthew's version (20:20–8) it is the mother of the sons of Zebedee who made the request on their behalf. She came to Jesus with her sons and kneeling before him she asked him for something. She was a disciple herself, one of the 'many women' who accompanied Jesus on that last stage of his journey south to Jerusalem; and she was one of those who witnessed from afar the crucifixion. It is a small example of how family ambition – in this case a mother's ambition for her sons – can be so potentially divisive in a team. The warning signs were already there: 'When the ten heard it, they were indignant at the two brothers.' If Jesus had acceded to her request it would have split the Twelve irrevocably into two factions. Yet Jesus' skilful reply avoided the risk of humiliating the brothers or their mother in front of the group with an outright rejection of their request.

Although this incident stands alone it does suggest that Jesus was no believer in the principle of 'divide-and-rule'. Doubtless with the help of Simon Peter, Jesus maintained the unity and harmony of the Twelve and the avid company of disciples and adherents who followed him. But it was not always easy, hence the teaching on leadership that we shall explore later.

As I have suggested, the centripetal forces in a group holding it together as a cohesive unity are opposed by centrifugal forces pushing it towards disintegration. Hostility or opposition between two individual members, or between a small clique and the rest, works centrifugally. The strength or weakness of the common *task* is a factor here, for the three needs present in working groups – *task*, *team* and *individual* – are interactive as if in three overlapping circles. The imminence of the 'kingdom of God' as the disciples walked towards Jerusalem seems to have weakened their unity. Moreover, their common task was weak in the sense that it was about to end. Unlike Jesus, they lacked the natural gifts and knowledge of the scriptures needed to preach or teach – still less dispute – among the scribes in the Temple. What else could they do except hang about like unemployed labourers and speculate about the 'kingdom of God'? And, as the proverb says, the Devil finds work for idle hands.

A Lost Sheep – Judas Iscariot

Setting aside for the moment the idea of Satan-possession, just why Judas Iscariot gradually or suddenly became disaffected and in effect left the Twelve in order to betray Jesus is a mystery. But in the context of a book on the leadership of Jesus, it raises an issue that cannot be sidestepped: did Jesus as a leader fail over Judas?

It is best to start with the facts, such as we have them. Jesus was sitting in the house of Simon the leper in the village of Bethany. A woman entered and proceeded to pour over his head the contents of an alabaster flask of a specially valuable kind of fragrant ointment. In the Gospel of John's account (12:1–8), the woman was identified as Mary of Bethany and there she is said to have anointed the feet rather than the head of Jesus and wiped them with her hair.

The fact that Jesus accepted such an act caused indignation in 'some' (Mark), 'the disciples' (Matthew) or 'Judas' (John).

By any of these accounts, it is clear that not everything Jesus said or did was agreeable to his followers. The issue here seems to have been the waste of money, for this kind of the rare ointment imported from India was worth 300 silver denarii, and a single denarius could buy a sheep. It could have been sold, they reasoned, and the money given to the poor. The anger of the disciples seems to have been directed against the woman: 'And they reproached her.' Was it not a law of 'the kingdom of God' that everything beyond the barest essentials of life should be given away to the needy neighbour?

'Let her alone; why do you trouble her?' replied Jesus. 'She has done a beautiful thing to me' (Mark 14:5–6). Grace knows how to receive as well as give, and so his words may have come from a sensitive spirit. On the other hand, Messiah means 'Anointed' and this act may have been 'beautiful' in that it is the only time that Jesus was anointed – perhaps by one who believed he was indeed the Messiah.

Why did Judas alone not accept Jesus' explanation of the act? John's Gospel says that Judas had protested against the cost of the ointment not because he cared for the poor, 'but because he was a thief, and as he had the money box he used to take what was put into it'. Straight away after the incident, as if it were cause and effect, Judas 'went to the chief priests in order to betray him to them' (Mark 14:10). In return for information for a suitable opportunity to seize Jesus in the absence of the crowds, the priests promised him money. Matthew alone relates (26:15) that there and then Judas received a down payment of thirty silver pieces.

Was avarice the real motive of Judas? Or did he totally misinterpret what he had just seen? On an earlier occasion he had heard Jesus speak with warm approval of a widow he had seen putting her last farthings into the Treasury box in the Temple. Her generosity was great, measured not by the sum itself but against her available means. But she gave her substance to God, whereas this woman lavished a vastly greater sum – perhaps her whole substance – on the best ointment to pour over the head or feet of Jesus. Did Judas imagine that Jesus was accepting something akin to an act of worship? We shall never know.

If these accounts are accepted as historical, Jesus sensed the disaffection in Judas. There is a reference to Judas dipping his bread in the bowl with Jesus (Mark 14:20). If he had done so at the same time it would have been bad manners, and a sign perhaps of diminished respect. But did Jesus talk to Judas or go after him like a shepherd seeking a straying sheep? Again, we shall never know. It seems, however, as if Jesus would do nothing to protect himself. Judas continued to come and go. Even though Jesus knew intuitively that Judas had changed – and commented on it – there is no record that he took any action.

Judas may have been already the least popular figure among the Twelve. His function as treasurer may have contributed to his unpopularity. Moreover, Simon, James and John did constitute an inner ring among the Twelve, and it is possible that Judas felt excluded. Perhaps it is not only on account of his later infamy that his name always comes last in lists of the Twelve.

Judas' sudden and untimely death at the time of the crucifixion – perhaps from a heart attack or stroke – may have received a negative interpretation as proof of his guilt and a divine punishment. In Matthew's Gospel it is described as a suicide. For the disciples he may have been made into a scapegoat for their own failure to safeguard Jesus. Whether or not Judas betrayed Jesus by acting as a guide to the arresting party of soldiers is debatable. As Jesus himself pointed out to them, they could have arrested him at any time in the Temple where he had been teaching daily without the need to employ such a large force.

Smite the shepherd and the sheep will scatter. It is most probable that the Jewish authorities hoped that the execution of Jesus would lead to the disintegration of the company that had gathered around him. It had worked with John the Baptizer, why not Jesus? The answer is that Jesus had created a team. Moreover, it survived intact (except for Judas Iscariot) and stayed together under the leadership of Simon Peter. Not only did that team recover from the shock of the crucifixion but, imbued with the spirit of Jesus, and with renewed hope, it resolved to take up again the common work of proclaiming the 'good news' of the 'kingdom of God'. And they bore a new message about the role and person of Jesus as the one whom God had raised from the dead, one who would shortly return from heaven to lead in his kingdom. As a result, defeat was turned into victory. Jesus may have fallen and died like a seed in the ground as he had predicted, but a host of 'fellow-workers' sprang up from the ploughed earth to change the world. You can kill a man, but a true vision never dies.

7

The Vision of Jesus

Vision is the art of seeing things invisible.
Jonathan Swift

Jesus was a man with a vision – the 'kingdom of God on earth'. Like the smile of the Cheshire Cat in Lewis Carroll's tale, it remains visible long after Jesus had faded from sight. It too would fade into the background as Christianity developed, but it would never disappear. For the sayings and parables of the 'kingdom of God' are caught for ever in the amber of the Gospels. Still today it is a vision that speaks to people, especially those who are drawn to Jesus and discover his purpose for themselves.

The idea that the 'kingdom of God on earth' can function as a leadership vision in this way may seem strange. For the implication of the concept, taken at face value, is that God would shortly introduce his 'kingdom' in some supernatural and cosmic way – something, of course, that we know did not happen. How can this apparently 'false prophecy' serve as a leadership vision – one that a leader embraces and invites others to help him realize? To answer this question we must begin with the concept or vision itself. What did it actually mean to Jesus and his contemporaries?

The Kingdom of God on Earth

If Jesus was not the author of the concept of the 'kingdom of God', neither was John the Baptizer upon whose lips we find the phrase for the first time in the Christian Gospels (Matthew 3:2). Both men proclaimed the 'good news' that the 'kingdom of God' was *near* or *at hand*, but neither of them ever said plainly what it was. There is no explicit definition or description.

It is like finding an ancient scroll in a Dead Sea cave that is reduced to barely legible fragments, which we have to piece together and decipher as best we can.

One of the prominent characteristics of Semitic languages which enables us to group them together are three-consonant word roots common to them all. Vowel sounds were not indicated in the earliest form of writing. *Mlk*, which appears for example in Arabic as *malik*, king, is a good example. Our word *kingdom* translates the Greek word in turn used for the Aramaic *malkūt*. Only in quite isolated instances in the Jewish scriptures does *malkūt* denote a realm in the spatial sense of a territory with boundaries; almost always it stands for the government, authority or power of a king. The 'kingdom of God', then, is the effective rule of God – whatever that may mean.

The actual phrase 'kingdom of God' does not appear in the Hebrew scriptures. But it can be found in the *Targums*, as the various Aramaic translations or paraphrases of the scriptures are known. In addition it occurs in later rabbinic biblical commentaries and also in the Jewish liturgy. The expression 'kingdom of heaven' is even more common in these sources, as it enabled the more reverential writers to avoid using the name of God in any form. For this reason Matthew – the most 'Jewish' of the Gospels – has it no less than thirteen times.

If, as Luke's Gospel records, John the Baptizer's father was named Zechariah, it would be poetically appropriate. For the prophet Zechariah was the chief source for the contemporary belief that in the great day God would establish his 'kingdom' on earth: 'And the Lord will become king over all the earth on that day' (14:9). The *Targum* on these words contained the phrase 'kingdom of God'. What John the Baptizer and Jesus, together with their disciples, announce is that this prophecy of Zechariah is about to be fulfilled. The order of the kingdom of heaven, where God reigns, is soon to be replicated here on earth.

Why was the message of John and Jesus so revolutionary? As a modern parable, I suggest it had the effect of *zero-basing* the religion of the Jews. Zero-basing is a metaphor from the world of finance: it refers to a budgeting process in which each item is costed anew, rather than in relation to its size or status in the previous budget. In other words, the concept of the imminent arrival of the 'kingdom of God' as a new order replacing the old allowed the creative minds of Jesus and others to look with fresh eyes on every aspect of the religion of their day. Like the master of the household who brings out of his treasure what is new and what is old (Matthew 13:52), the scribe 'trained for the kingdom of heaven' will not just assume that the old wine of the Jewish religion could be poured into the new wineskins. Everything had to be assessed anew in the dawn light of the 'kingdom of God'. On these matters Jesus taught with an authority hitherto unencountered in Israel. And, as the proverb already quoted says, authority flows to the one who knows.

Developing the Vision

As a general principle the Semitic mind was far more concrete and less given to abstractions than the Greek mind. The distinction in modern literature between prose and poetry is difficult to apply to the Bible, for some of the recognizable hallmarks of traditional Western poetry – metre and rhyme – are not there. Yet the teaching of Jesus falls towards the poetic end of the spectrum. There is a terseness of style, a richness of figurative language, sometimes an ambiguity of meaning, and the words used demand a response from the listener. The parables so characteristic of Jesus (Mark 4:33–4) clearly fall within these parameters. The Semitic (and poetic) concreteness of imagery is one of their hallmarks.

Consequently, the 'kingdom of God' in the parables told by Jesus sounds as if he were talking about an actual place, not some abstract ideal as that which we encounter in Plato's *Republic* or Thomas More's *Utopia*. In seven parables the 'kingdom of God', for example, is compared to a *house*, while in six others the focus is on a great festive *feast* that takes place in such a house. The 'kingdom' can be *entered* or not *entered* (Mark 9:47); one can *sit down* in it; people can *eat and drink* in it (Luke 22:30). A man may *be not far from* the 'kingdom of God' (Mark 12:34). It has a *door* or *gate* on which one can knock and which may be locked (Matthew 25:1–12). Thus it was like a *house* or *walled city*, a mirror image of Satan's domain (Mark 3:23–5; Matthew 12:25). Men are said to *take it by force* (Matthew 11:12; Luke 16:16). The Greek word used here is *biazesthai*, which described attackers storming a city.

Figurative language such as this would have made the concept of the 'kingdom of God' graspable and intelligible to the Semitic minds of the Galileans and others who heard Jesus. He ran the risk, however, that his hearers would take it too literally – remember the wrangle of the disciples over the seating-plan at the *feast*. As we have seen, *malkūt* in the Bible means reign or rule, not a king's domain in the more physical sense. Perhaps we come closest to a definition in Matthew's version of the prayer that Jesus gave to his disciples (6:10):

> Thy kingdom come,
> Thy will be done,
> On earth as it is in heaven.

Here we can probably assume that the second petition extended or echoed the theme of the first (compare, for example Psalm 104:28). It was not walls or boundaries that delineated the 'kingdom of God'; it was present where God's will was obeyed on earth as spontaneously, completely and joyfully as it was by those who actually saw God and lived in his presence. But what is the will of God? The answer to that question depends upon our vision of the nature of God.

One striking way in which Jesus creatively developed the vision of the 'kingdom of God' concerns this figure of God. The awe-ful vision of God as a king enthroned in glory high above his heavenly court was at hand in the scriptures (see, for example, Isaiah 6), but that image of God is largely noticeable by its absence in the teaching of Jesus. The God of the parables is often the owner of a large estate, a *pater familias* with a household of grown-up sons and hired servants working his lands and vineyards. Jesus characteristically spoke of God as Father, or *Abba* in Aramaic, which suggests a much closer and more personal relationship than, say, a subject in Galilee to the emperor Tiberius in Rome. It is doubtful if Jesus ever met a real king or saw a royal court, whereas he knew at first hand the estates and large households of Galilee. Doing the will of this God was less a matter of obeying the ordinances of an all-powerful king, backed by the sanctions of reward and punishment, and more like lovingly emulating the generous goodness of the Creator and Father of humankind.

The Law of the Kingdom

One of the characteristics of both a great leader and a great teacher – Jesus was both – is the ability to simplify complexity. Such a leader can discern the elements in a complex situation, and then present them as the essentials. As Einstein once said, 'Everything should be made as simple as possible, but not more simple.' By the time of Jesus, the Law of Moses had become quite complex: one scribe counted 365 negative commands and 248 positive ones within its bounds. Nor was the ever-growing body of explanatory material an aid to simplicity. It was part of the genius of Jesus as a spiritual leader to reduce this complex Law of Moses to a single principle composed of two related essentials:

> One of the scribes came up and heard them disputing with one another, and seeing that he answered them well, asked him, 'Which commandment is the first of all?' Jesus answered, 'The first is, "Hear, O Israel: the Lord our God, the Lord is one; and you shall love the Lord your God with all your heart, and with all your soul, and with all your mind, and with all your strength." The second is this, "You shall love your neighbour as yourself." There is no other commandment greater than these.' And the scribe said to him, 'You are right, Teacher; you have truly said that he is one, and there is no other but he; and to love him with all the heart, and with all the understanding, and with all the strength, and to love one's neighbour as oneself, is much more than all whole burnt offerings and sacrifices.' And when Jesus saw that he answered wisely, he said to him, 'You are not far from the kingdom of God.' (Mark 12:28–34)

That last sentence suggests that the two elements or essentials – yoked by *love* – are the twin pillars of the 'kingdom of God'. By coupling together Deuteronomy 6:5 and Leviticus 19:18 in this way, Jesus succeeded in integrating in one principle all the theological and ethical content of the Torah. It is an astonishing achievement.

The scribe, however, put a supplementary question: 'And who is my neighbour?' Jesus gave in reply the famous parable of a wayfaring Samaritan. It reveals how Jesus could take the bare message of John the Baptizer – 'He who has two coats, let him share with him who has none, and he who has food, let him do likewise' – and clothe it in an unforgettable story. A priest and a Levite both pass by a victim of robbers as he lies wounded and destitute by the road, but a Samaritan takes him up and cares for him at an inn. Which of the three was neighbour to the man?

The sheer generosity of the love which God expects and admires – the will of God – is brought out even more strongly than in Luke in the version of the story that appears in the *Gospel of Barnabas* (see Note 2). In it the compassionate Samaritan not only 'washed his wounds with wine and anointed them with oil' and then bound them up as in Luke, but he also 'comforted' the victim in his emotional distress. Then he set the now conscious man on his own horse until they reached the inn. Next morning the Samaritan gave the victim four gold pieces or *aureii* (as compared to the two silver *denarii* in Luke's version), a sum worth above 100 *denarii*. Incidentally, the small detail in *Barnabas* that the Samaritan handed the money to the wounded man to give to the host, not the host himself as in Luke, is an authentic touch in those days of dishonest inn-keepers. Lastly, the account in *Barnabas* alone includes these parting words of comfort and cheer to the victim: 'Be of good heart, for I will speedily return and conduct you to my own home.'

Entering the Kingdom

The parable of the wayfaring Samaritan was even more powerful given the fact that no love was lost between the Jews and their neighbours in Samaria. It was an ancient family quarrel. The Jews looked down on the Samaritans as the bastard offspring of inter-marriages between Jews and Gentiles in the days of the Exile, while the Samaritans for their part regarded themselves as guardians of the true religion of Moses. If a Samaritan could be closer to the 'kingdom of God' than a priest of the Temple or a Levite, then it was as if the 'kingdom of God' had open frontiers. The children of Abraham had the privilege of being the first to be invited to enter it, but if they refused to do so God would make up the numbers from the likes of the good Samaritan.

The fact that Jesus lived in Galilee helps us to understand his transcendent vision of the 'kingdom of God'. Mainly on account of its geographical situation, the people of Galilee developed a distinctive sub-culture of their own. They had a sense of being Galileans, different from their southern neighbours in Judaea. They spoke a dialect of Aramaic which the southerners could find hard to understand, slurring their guttural sounds together. In the Talmud, for example, there is a story of a Galilean shouting out his wares for sale in the streets of Jerusalem, and being stopped by passers-by to be asked if he was selling *wool* or *wine*, a *sheep* or a *donkey*! They also dropped consonants and vowels at the end of words, so that, for instance, Jesus' Aramaic name *Yesua* – a shortened form of *Yehosua* (Joshua) – would become *Yesu* or *Jesu*.

In fact the Jews in Galilee were culturally in much the same situation as their kinsfolk in the diaspora, even though they lived only some one hundred miles from Jerusalem. For Galilee was a natural cradle for a new religion that would one day embrace both Jews and Gentiles.

Galilee in Aramaic meant 'the Territory', and it was so called in much the same way as early Americans might refer to the 'Frontier'. Its full name was 'the Galilee (or Territory) of the Gentiles' (Matthew 4:15). The Gentiles in question were mainly the descendants of various indigenous Semitic peoples – the old

Canaanites – as well as incomers from Syria. The region had been conquered (or reconquered) by the Jews only a few hundred years before the days of Jesus, with many of the inhabitants being forcibly converted to the Jewish religion. Moreover, its somewhat remote geographical position in the north, astride some main trade routes from east to west, made Galilee into an enclave for its Jewish inhabitants. The Jews could not anyway have numbered more than half the population of several millions. The relatively cosmopolitan nature of Galilee may have suited Herod Antipas, whose father was an Idumaean and his mother a Samaritan.

The Galilee Jews saw rather more of the Samaritans than their Judaean brethren. For there were two routes for the annual pilgrimage to Jerusalem: one down the Jordan valley and up through the hills by way of Jericho; the other – shorter and more direct – lying through Samaria. Consequently they may have known them more as individuals, good and less good like the rest of us. Certainly Jesus saw them that way. For example, entering a village 'between Samaria and Galilee' Jesus responded to the pleas of ten lepers and healed them. After they had, on his instruction, gone to show themselves to the priests and were made 'clean' on the way, only one turned back, 'praising God with a loud voice.' He prostrated himself at Jesus' feet and thanked him. And 'he was a Samaritan' (Luke 17:11–19).

As with the Samaritans, so with the Semitic Gentiles of the region. They, too, could 'enter the kingdom of God'. Jesus, for example, healed a Gentile centurion's favourite slave. 'I tell you,' he said of the centurion to the multitude that followed him, 'not even in Israel have I found such faith' (Luke 7:1–9). On another occasion he at first rebuffed a Syrophoenician woman who came to him for help when he walked in the region of Tyre: 'Let the children be fed first, for it is not fair to take the children's food and throw it to the dogs.' She replied, 'Sir, even the dogs under the table eat the crumbs.' When Jesus discerned in her such quick intelligence, faith and humility, he granted her request (Matthew 15:21–8; Mark 7:24–30).

The 'kingdom of God' then, as it developed in the mind of Jesus, transcended the religious, social and national divisions of his day. The rejection of the 'good news' by his fellow Jews would only strengthen in time this tendency, already present in Jesus, to open its gates to others whatever their race, tradition or background.

> He went on his way through towns and villages, teaching, and journeying toward Jerusalem. And some one said to him, 'Lord, will those who are saved be few?' And he said to them, 'Strive to enter by the narrow door; for many, I tell you, will seek to enter and will not be able. When once the householder has risen up and shut the door, you will begin to stand outside and to knock at the door, saying, "Lord, open to us." He will answer you, "I do not know where you come from." Then you will begin to say, "We ate and drank in your presence, and you taught in our streets." But he will say, "I tell you, I do not know where you come from; depart from me, all you workers of iniquity!" And you will weep and gnash your teeth, when you see Abraham and Isaac and Jacob and all the prophets in the kingdom of God and you yourselves thrust out. And men will come from east and west, and from north and south, and sit at table in the kingdom of God. And behold, some are last who will be first, and some are first who will be last.' (Luke 13:22–30)

Thus the invitation to enter the 'kingdom of God' can be refused like an *invitation* to a feast (Luke 14:15–24). The *opportunity* to enter it can be lost, as the parable of the foolish bridesmaids taught (Matthew 25:1–13). And the *privilege* of entering the 'kingdom' can be taken away (Matthew 8:11–12, 21:43; Luke 13:28).

The necessary conditions for *entry* into the 'kingdom of God' in the Gospels are in fact accessible to all people, be they from east or west, north or south. They include a *childlike spirit* (Matthew 18:4) a *forgiving spirit* (Matthew 18:23–35), a *certain attitude to one's fellow humans* (Matthew 25:31–46), and a *certain standard of righteousness* (Matthew 5:20). Hindrances to *entry* included *riches* (Mark 10:23–5) and *lack of commitment* (Luke 9:26–7).

'The kingdom of God is in the midst of you'

People are bidden to *seek* the 'kingdom of God'. The word for *seek* is *zetein* in Greek, and it can be translated as 'make it the object of all your endeavours'. It seems paradoxical to be told both to *wait* in patience for the 'kingdom of God' to come as God's act and yet to *seek* it in this wholehearted and dedicated way.

In the Semitic culture of Jesus the only way that reality can be indicated is as an act of God. By saying that God would bring in the 'kingdom' *soon* or that it was *at hand* Jesus was in fact seeking to convey the *reality* of the vision in the only way that Semitic culture allowed. It was no desert mirage. Even though we cannot see or touch it, this is more real than the world as it appears today. Therefore, live now according to that reality. For those who truly accept that message, the 'kingdom of God' is already present, already at work. For those with eyes to see, it is unfolding around them.

> Being asked by the Pharisees when the kingdom of God was coming, he answered them, 'The kingdom of God is not coming with signs to be observed; nor will they say, "Lo, here it is!" or "There!" for behold, the kingdom of God is in the midst of you.' (Luke 17:20–1)

As a modern parable, the concept of the 'kingdom of God' is like light. Light's electrons appear to be composed of both waves and particles. These properties are incompatible, yet both have been detected. It seems to depend on one's perspective at the time, on what questions one puts to the phenomenon. So the 'kingdom of God' is something in the hand of God, something that he may or may not establish at some point known to him in the future. It is also present and active now, something that men and women and children can bear witness to and serve in their lives.

At the beginning of this chapter I called the 'kingdom of God' a *leadership* vision. For without vision no real change can enter history; no significant progress can be made. As humans we have the capacity to imagine a better future, and that is the first step to change. It is a function of leaders to have vision in this way. Vision gives us a sense of direction, something to work towards. Vision is like a constellation of stars by which the helmsman steers the ship, not a destination that will one day be reached – at least in this world as we know it.

Life without such a notable vision is drudgery, but a vision without a task is merely a dream mirage. Jesus *seeks* the 'kingdom of God' with every fibre of his being. He worked immensely hard himself, and he called others to share the same arduous labour. 'We must work the works of him who sent me,' he told them, 'while it is day; night comes, when no one can work' (John 9:4). But Jesus did more than surpass even John the Baptizer in journeys, miracles and teaching – he *lived* the vision so that others could see it in his life.

Living the Vision

> You are the light of the world. A city set on a hill cannot be hid. Nor do men light a lamp and put it under a bushel, but on a stand, and it gives light to all in the house. Let your light so shine before men, that they may see your good works and give glory to your Father who is in heaven. (Matthew 5:14–16)

From these words it is clear that Jesus expected his disciples to live the vision of the 'kingdom of God' and thereby fulfil their calling. In what ways did Jesus do so himself? One salient example is compassion, the quality that the good Samaritan in the parable possessed but was apparently lacking in the hearts of the priest and Levite. Jesus was said to be moved by compassion on a number of occasions (Mark 1:41, 6:34, 8:2, 9:22; Matthew 9:36, 14:14, 15:32). His visit to the village or town of Nain in Galilee gives us a vivid example of his compassion – sympathy that moves into action – at work:

> Soon afterward he went to a city called Nain, and his disciples and a great crowd went with him. As he drew near to the gate of the city, behold, a man who had died was being carried

out, the only son of his mother, and she was a widow; and a large crowd from the city was with her. And when the Lord saw her, he had compassion on her and said to her, 'Do not weep.' And he came and touched the bier, and the bearers stood still. And he said, 'Young man, I say to you, arise.' And the dead man sat up, and began to speak. And he gave him to his mother. Fear seized them all; and they glorified God, saying, 'A great prophet has arisen among us!' and 'God has visited his people!' And this report concerning him spread through the whole of Judea and all the surrounding country. (Luke 7:11–17)

Real compassion is always costly. In the case of Jesus, his compassionate response to the Gentiles who beseeched him to heal them, their relatives or servants may have had one unforeseen and unfortunate consequence. According to the *Gospel of Barnabas* the belief that Jesus was a god in human form spread first among the Roman soldiery as a result of his miraculous healings. If so, it is ironic that a detachment of them should be called upon to crucify Jesus. A trace of this tradition may have found its way into Mark's Gospel where it is related that the centurion on duty at Golgotha, seeing that Jesus had stopped breathing, said, 'Truly this man was a son of God' (Mark 15:39, NEB). This exclamation, of course, may have been no more than a soldier's tribute to the extraordinary courage and endurance of Jesus on the cross in face of certain death – a quality, as I have said, greatly admired by the Romans. But, alternatively, it may have been an echo of a belief among Pilate's Gentile soldiers that Jesus was a god. Later, both Peter and Paul on occasion had to take steps to avoid being worshipped as gods on account of their miraculous healing powers (Acts 10:25–6, 14:11–18). The belief among the Roman soldiers that Jesus was a god may have fuelled the charge of blasphemy levelled against Jesus by his fellow Jews, possibly the principal charge that led ultimately to his execution.

Compassion is an expression of the presence of the 'kingdom of God' in a person, Jesus taught, because God himself is compassionate. The younger son who squandered his fortune and returned to his father's estate in trepidation received a very different greeting from the one he feared. 'His father saw him and had compassion, and ran and embraced him and kissed him' (Luke 15:20). If God is compassionate in this way, we are left to draw the implication for ourselves. 'Be merciful, even as your Father is merciful' (Luke 6:36).

One of Jesus' most distinctive teachings was his command to love one's enemies. Luke's version (6:27–8) preserves the poetic structure of the original Aramaic couplet:

Love your enemies, do good to those who hate you,
bless those who curse you, pray for those who abuse you.

As a principle it seems to run clean counter to the 'natural law' of equivalence in reciprocal exchanges: what you receive is balanced by what you give. For example, if someone hates you, you hate them; if they kill one of your family, you kill one of theirs. 'Revenge is a kind of wild justice,' wrote Francis Bacon, and by 'wild' he meant 'natural'. One of the *new* 'treasures' of the 'kingdom of God' was the extension of generous love and compassionate action to the enemy whose antagonism has shown itself towards one in hatred or destructive attitude or hostile action. But did Jesus live the demanding vision when it came to 'loving' – doing good in return for evil – to those who showed him ill-will or enmity?

There is, of course, the great prayer on the cross recorded only in Luke's Gospel (23:34): 'Father, forgive them; for they know not what they do.' Whether or not Jesus actually said these words, they must have reflected a tradition as to what sort of man he was. This is the kind of prayer he *would* have uttered if pain, thirst and other suffering had allowed him to speak. In a lower register, there is one instance of Jesus forgiving his enemies in one of the fragments of the early Syrian Christian tradition which come to us by courtesy of Muslim editors:

The Messiah passed by a company of Jews, who cursed him, but he blessed them. It was said to him: 'They speak you evil and you speak them well!' He answered: 'Everyone spends of that which he has.'

There is another possible example in Luke's account of Jesus' last journey to Jerusalem, which, according to him, lay through Samaria (although that does not tie up with the visit to Jericho where blind Bartimaeus was healed):

> When the days drew near for him to be received up, he set his face to go to Jerusalem. And he sent messengers ahead of him, who went and entered a village of the Samaritans, to make ready for him; but the people would not receive him, because his face was set toward Jerusalem. And when his disciples James and John saw it, they said, 'Lord, do you want us to bid fire come down from heaven and consume them?' But he turned and rebuked them. And they went on to another village. (Luke 9:51–6)

Some ancient manuscripts follow the rebuke of Jesus with these telling words: 'You do not know what manner of spirit you are of, for the Son of Man came not to destroy men's lives but to save them.'

These instances few as they are, suggest that Jesus was no hypocrite: he practised what he preached. Leadership *is* example. Not only did Jesus transform the bare expectation of the 'kingdom of God' into a compelling vision, but he also lived it. In retrospect, his disciples would for ever associate the 'kingdom of God' or its equivalent 'eternal life' (Matthew 19:16) with the spirit that was in Jesus. Apart from his spirit, Jesus also left them a legacy of teaching and example on how they, in their turn, should exercise a similar leadership among their fellow-workers for the 'kingdom of God'.

It is the example of Jesus as well as his words that draws men and women to the way of love he pioneered. To those who respond he is still the 'chief leader' (Greek *archegos*, author, leader-in-chief, pioneer – Acts 3:15, 5:31; Hebrews 2:10, 12:2) on that journey, be it universal, corporate or personal. An *archegos* is the one who is both source or initiator and leader, the one who takes the first action and then brings those on whose behalf he has acted to the intended goal. Paul wrote to the Philippians:

> If there is any encouragement in Christ, any incentive of love, any participation in the Spirit, any affection and sympathy, complete my joy by being of the same mind, having the same love, being in full accord and of one mind. Do nothing from selfishness or conceit, but in humility count others better than yourselves. Let each of you look not only to his own interests, but also to the interests of others. Have this mind among yourselves, which you have in Christ Jesus . . . (Philippians 2:1–5)

8

Serve to Lead

Do not, as some ungracious pastors do,
Show me the steep and thorny way to heaven,
Whiles, like a puff'd and reckless libertine,
Himself the primrose path of dalliance treads,
And recks not his own rede [advice].
William Shakespeare, *Hamlet*

The most distinctive aspect of Jesus' teaching on leadership is
his emphasis that a leader is essentially a servant. The two Greek
words that are used in his sayings on servanthood are *doulos*
and *diakonos*. Can they be distinguished? On the whole *doulos*,
which means 'servant' or 'slave', is used when the emphasis is
on the task, the accountability, on being under authority and
obeying orders. As we have seen, Jesus balances it with the idea
of being a friend, yoke-fellow, partner – one who knows and
shares the common vision. Where the emphasis falls on the
giving of personal service, or the stress is on the spirit of love
and humility which should inspire the service of others, then
diakonos is more frequently used.

The word *diakonos*, servant, means literally 'to wait at table',
to render service during a meal. This sense occurs in Jesus'
parable where the servant is ordered by his master to prepare
the supper and serve it (Luke 17:8), and also in the surprising
story (Luke 12:37) of the master who reverses the roles and
thanks the faithful servants by waiting on them himself.

Teaching on Humility

The figure of the servant *diakonos* exemplified humility. For
example, Mark recorded one of several arguments among the
disciples on the question of who was the greatest among them,

this time on the road to Capernaum. The disciples seem to have been overwhelmed by embarrassment when Jesus asked them what they had been discussing.

> And they came to Capernaum; and when he was in the house he asked them, 'What were you discussing on the way?' But they were silent; for on the way they had discussed with one another who was the greatest. And he sat down and called the twelve; and he said to them, 'If any one would be first, he must be last of all and servant of all.' (Mark 9:33–5)

To be a 'servant of all' meant that no distinctions would be made as to whom one should serve or not serve. Such servanthood implied an unqualified availability to all who have need of one's service.

Then Jesus 'took a child, and put him in the midst of them' as an illustration of the kind of humble attitude God expected in a leader. In Matthew's parallel account Jesus says, 'Whoever humbles himself like this child, he is the greatest in the kingdom of heaven' (Matthew 18:4). Luke's version (9:46–8) concludes with the statement: 'He who is least among you all is the one who is great.'

When the similar dispute broke out over who should have the places of honour at the right and left hand of Jesus (Matthew 20:20–8; Mark 10:35–40), Jesus in reply contrasted the domineering rule of the Gentile authorities with the new kind of leadership he expected among his disciples. As he said to them: 'Whoever would be great among you must be your servant' (Matthew 20:26). Then, according to Mark, Jesus cited his own example: 'For the Son of Man also came not to be served but to serve, and to give his life as a ransom for many' (10:45).

Luke records yet a third argument on the same issue of personal greatness among the Twelve, this time following the Last Supper. As in Matthew 20, Jesus contrasts the conduct of the client kings of Rome with the servant leadership he has in mind. He refers to their arrogance and their custom of making benefactions to Greek cities and cult centres, just as Augustus himself did. Josephus confirms Herod the Great's largesse to Greek cities, an example followed by his descendants. These acts of philantropy in support of Greek culture and its pagan temples were deeply inimical to the religion of the Jews.

> The kings of the Gentiles exercise lordship over them; and those in authority over them are called benefactors. But not so with you; rather let the greatest among you become as the youngest, and the leader [*ho hegemenos*] as one who serves [*ho diakonon*]. For which is the greater, one who sits at table, or one who serves? Is it not the one who sits at table? But I am among you as one who serves. (Luke 22:25–7)

As Jesus had just finished washing the disciples' feet (and according to one manuscript kissing them), the picture of his own humble service to them was fresh in their minds. Jesus was not discouraging those who aspired to lead, but merely showing them what true leadership entails.

Jesus, in fact, was not alone in sensing the negative nuances in the concept of lordship, its overtones of despotic and overbearing control over others deemed inferiors. No less a person than Augustus Caesar himself detested the word, as his biographer Suetonius writes:

> He always abhorred the title of Lord, as ill-omened and offensive. And when, in a play, performed at the theatre, at which he was present, these words were introduced, 'O just and gracious lord', and the whole company, with joyful acclamations, testified their approbation of them, as applied to him, he instantly put a stop to their indecent flattery, by waving his hands, and frowning sternly, and next day publicly declared his displeasure in a proclamation. He never afterwards would suffer himself to be addressed in that manner, even by his own children or grandchildren, either in jest or in earnest, and forbade them the use of all such complimentary expressions to one another. He rarely entered any city or town, or departed from it, except in the evening or night, to avoid giving any person the trouble of complimenting him.

It was not only the worst of the Gentile kings who 'lorded it' over their fellows. Josephus mentioned the haughty attitude of the aristocratic Sadducees: 'The Pharisees are friendly to one another and seek to promote concord with the general public, but the Sadducees, even towards each other, show a more dis-agreeable spirit, and in their relations with their fellow-countrymen they are harsh as they might be to foreigners.' If the Gospels can be believed on this score, some of the Pharisees showed a similar spirit to the Sadducees. Jesus denounced them for their hypocrisy – 'they preach but do not practice' – as well as their preoccupation with outward appearance at the expense of inner reality:

> They do all their deeds to be seen by men; for they make their phylacteries broad and their fringes long, and they love the place of honour at feasts and the best seats in the syna-gogues, and salutations in the market places, and being called rabbi by men. But you are not to be called rabbi . . . And call no man your father . . . Neither be called masters . . . He who is greatest among you shall be your servant; whoever exalts himself will be humbled, and whoever humbles himself will be exalted.' (Matthew 23:5–12)

Taking the lowest place at the table, Jesus taught, was the outward sign of one who saw himself as a servant, not a master. At one feast on a Sabbath, which Jesus and his disciples attended as guests of a ruler who belonged to the Pharisees, he noticed – observant as always – how those invited chose the places of honour at the table. Presumably Jesus' disciples were among these status-seeking guests, for he told this parable:

> When you are invited by any one to a marriage feast, do not sit down in a place of honour, lest a more eminent man than you be invited by him; and he who invited you both will come and say to you, 'Give place to this man,' and then you will begin with shame to take the lowest place. But when you are invited, go and sit in the lowest place, so that when your host comes he may say to you, 'Friend, go up higher'; then

you will be honoured in the presence of all who sit at table with you. For every one who exalts himself will be humbled, and he who humbles himself will be exalted. (Luke 14:8–11)

How Jesus Exemplified Servant-Leadership

Jesus' symbolic act of washing his disciples' feet was an expression of his own humility. Who but a deeply humble man would reply thus to a greeting of a rich young man intent on acquiring salvation:

As he was setting out on his journey, a man ran up and knelt before him, and asked him, 'Good Teacher, what must I do to inherit eternal life?' And Jesus said to him, 'Why do you call me good? No one is good but God alone.' (Mark 10:17–18)

Nor did Jesus 'lord it' over his disciples. Although Jesus could be tough or demanding as a leader, there was nothing harsh, overbearing or domineering in his manner towards them. He saw himself primarily as a servant of God and then as their servant in the manner of a shepherd or leader. The meekness and gentleness in Jesus' attitude to God overflowed into his relations with others. In his second letter to the Corinthians, Paul refers to the 'meekness and gentleness' of Jesus, which suggests that before the Gospels as we have them were compiled, Jesus was credited with these twin virtues.

Humility and meekness are like brother and sister. In Hebrew the word translated as 'meek' meant originally to bow low before God. The image of an energetic and spirited war horse, broken in and sensitive to the slightest touch of the bridle or its rider's knee, is the best image of what it means to be 'gentle' or 'meek'. It is the 'meek' in this sense – those who do God's will on earth in the spirit in which it is done in heaven – who are blessed by Jesus, 'for they shall inherit the earth' (Matthew 5:5, quoting Psalm 37:11). Gentleness in a leader is not a sign of weakness. It is the ability to use only the slightest force needed, and that in a tactful and considerate way.

The sensitivity of such humble and meek leaders to the light touch or the 'daughter of the voice' of God is replicated in their fine receptivity or responsiveness to others. Even in the press of the crowd that thronged about him, Jesus was aware of the woman who had suffered from haemorrhages for twelve years and who reached out to touch the hem of his garment:

> And Jesus said, 'Who was it that touched me?' When all denied it, Peter said, 'Master, the multitudes surround you and press upon you!' But Jesus said, 'Some one touched me; for I perceive that power has gone forth from me.' And when the woman saw that she was not hidden, she came trembling, and falling down before him declared in the presence of all the people why she had touched him, and how she had been immediately healed. And he said to her, 'Daughter, your faith has made you well; go in peace.' (Luke 8:45–8)

The story is a parable for leaders, because they too have a 'touching ministry'. For a good leader is sensitive to the 'touch' of others in the course of a busy day, the little unrecorded meetings or chance encounters in a corridor. Each one of these brief encounters in its small way is a 'moment of truth'. Each one, too, calls upon the leader's resources of time and energy. Yet 'touching' is a two-way process: leaders can also be inspired or uplifted by a word or spontaneous act.

The gentleness of Jesus and his openness as 'servant to all' to those who pressed in upon him are well illustrated by his blessing of the children.

> Then children were brought to him that he might lay his hands on them and pray. The disciples rebuked the people; but Jesus said, 'Let the children come to me, and do not hinder them; for to such belongs the kingdom of heaven.' And he laid his hands on them and went away. (Matthew 19:13–15)

The graceful tenderness of Jesus appears in this story. Perhaps, too, in it there is a prophetic sense that 'the kingdom of God' belonged to a new generation, to the young in spirit. Certainly it is true today that so often it is the sight of innocent children, with the uncreated future before them, that fuels the hope and dedication of those who work for the 'kingdom of God on earth'.

Jesus, then, mirrored the humility and gentleness of God. The divine force was as invisible and slight as the wind in a boat's sail on the Sea of Galilee, and yet it could move mountains and change people's granite hearts. In this spirit Jesus indeed stood in the line of David, who had praised God:

> Thou hast given me the shield of thy salvation,
> and thy gentleness made me great. (2 Samuel 22:36)

Sharing Equally the Hardships and Dangers

For Jesus, all those called by the 'good news' were servants of God, and he was among his fellow-servants – not over them – as their leader. Thus Jesus gave himself no special privileges. He walked with his disciples on the dusty roads, in sun or rain or wind, though doubtless he could have ridden on a horse or an ass, had he chosen to do so. According to early Syrian Christian tradition (arguably supported by his instructions to the Seventy) Jesus had only one tunic and he walked barefooted. He carried no provisions bag or purse of money. He slept where he slept. 'Foxes have holes and birds of the air have nests, but the Son of Man has nowhere to lay his head' (Matthew 8:20), he told one who aspired to accompany him. Many a night Jesus must have wrapped himself in a cloak and slept among his followers under the stars, perhaps like the patriarch Jacob using a rock for a pillow, just as Hannibal had once slept among his soldiers in his red cloak.

Most important of all, Jesus shared equally with the disciples whatever food or drink was available. It is possible that these shares of food – doubtless sometimes very small – took on an almost sacramental character. Blessed by thanksgiving to God, it may have seemed as if they miraculously satisfied hunger or thirst. In the desert Bedouin tribes, to eat bread and salt together was almost a sacred act of fellowship: the Arabic words for 'bread' and 'brotherhood' come from the same root.

Yet when it came to danger, as events would reveal in the case of Jesus, leaders face more than their fair share of it. After the death of John the Baptizer, Jesus must have known that he was more vulnerable than the disciples, just as a leader who goes in front of soldiers into battle is more likely to be killed than someone in the rank-and-file. Jesus was not fool-hardy, for on several occasions he withdrew from threatening situations, but neither did he go out of his way to protect himself.

The test of love is the willingness for self-sacrifice. Jesus taught that leadership is a form of love, and that it, too, should be ready to pay the ultimate price of giving one's life for others:

> I am the good shepherd. The good shepherd lays down his life for the sheep. He who is a hireling and not a shepherd, whose own the sheep are not, sees the wolf coming and leaves the sheep and flees; and the wolf snatches them and scatters them. He flees because he is a hireling and cares nothing for the sheep. (John 10:11–13)

As we know, Jesus as a shepherd or servant-leader did meet an early death. The Gospels insist that his crucifixion was a voluntary act, something undertaken and endured for the love of others. Whether or not Jesus died in this cruel way by his own choice, here at any rate is a leader who was willing to sacrifice himself to the common cause if the call came to him to do so.

'A disciple is not above his teacher, nor a servant above his master,' Jesus told his disciples (Matthew 10:24). Luke adds, 'but every one when he is fully taught will be like his teacher' (6:40). Both by his teaching and example, Jesus prepared his disciples to be leaders in his spirit, and many of them would, like their master, 'take up the cross'.

But Jesus' teaching on the spirit of leadership is universally applicable. Society and organizations in this world, as opposed to the 'kingdom of God', cannot exist without hierarchy. But the best leaders live and work as if they are among free and equal people. Lacking even a trace of arrogance, they lead by sheer ability and character – they are 'good shepherds'.

But the higher a man's reputation stands, so much the more humble-minded he ought to be; and furthermore, his eyes should be fixed on the good of the whole community rather than on his own personal advantage. . . . Love is without servility, as it is without arrogance. Love knows of no divisions, promotes no discord; all the works of love are done in perfect fellowship.

The First Letter of Clement to the Corinthians, *c.* AD 96

Part Three

The Legacy of Jesus' Leadership

9

On Vision

*I was not disobedient to the heavenly
vision . . .*

Paul of Tarsus (Acts 26:19)

In these pages I have suggested that the clues to Jesus as a leader
and to his teachings on the nature of leadership lie in his vision
of the 'kingdom of God'. Responding to the opportunity created
by John the Baptizer, Jesus took ownership of this vision and
made it his own. By his greatness as a teacher and by the example
of his own life and death – living the vision – Jesus made it real
to those contemporaries who had 'eyes to see and ears to hear'.

The story of what happened next to that vision as Christianity
slowly formed itself lies beyond the scope of this present book.
In brief, however, the concept of the 'kingdom of God' coming
on earth gradually faded into the background, to be replaced
by a much greater emphasis on the expiatory work of Christ
on the cross as the means whereby individuals might attain the
'eternal life' of Heaven. This world was viewed as no more than
a bridge over which Christians must travel before they crossed
the river of death and reached their goal – the Celestial City.

This gradual eclipse of the vision is not surprising. The mindset of the early church became predominantly Greek and Latin,
while the 'kingdom of God' and God's establishment of it on
earth were essentially Semitic ideas in their internal structure of
thought-form. To a logical Greek mind, the fact that the 'kingdom of God' had not appeared on cue, as it were, led to its
demotion in the cosmic drama.

Rediscovering the Vision of Jesus

Perhaps the greatest theological rediscovery of the last century is the original vision of Jesus, the first 'good news' or 'gospel' of the 'kingdom of God' and its *nearness* to us on earth. That rediscovery is for ever associated with the name of Albert Schweitzer. As an undergraduate in 1956, I was fortunate to catch sight of him when he came to Cambridge to receive an honorary degree.

The Jesus whom Schweitzer presented in a book published in 1906, best known by its English title *The Quest of the Historical Jesus*, is, as he said, a stranger to our times: 'the eschatological Jesus who lives expecting the end of the world and a supernatural kingdom of God'.

Schweitzer himself, it seems, retained a framework of the orthodox Lutheran belief he had acquired as a boy from his pastor father. In its framework, he accommodated the 'eschatogical Jesus' he had discerned. But Schweitzer sensed that the day of credal statements about Jesus was over. It is simply not required, he taught, that one should have an opinion about *who Jesus really was* – even Jesus himself had not asked that of his contemporaries. What then is required? Schweitzer's answer lay in the famous words that conclude his book:

> He comes to us as One unknown, without a name, as of old, by the lakeside, He came to those men who knew Him not. He speaks to us the same word: 'Follow thou me,' and sets us the tasks which He has to fulfil for our time. He commands. And to those who obey Him, whether they be wise or simple, He will reveal Himself in the toils, the conflicts, the suffering which they will pass through in His fellowship, and, as an ineffable mystery, they shall learn in their own experience Who He is.

Schweitzer was prepared to recognize that Jesus was capable of error, for 'the supernatural Kingdom of God, the manifestation of which He announced as imminent, did not appear'. But that made no difference to Schweitzer's own personal and

sacrificial commitment to the 'kingdom of God', which he interpreted in terms of love and compassionate action. In other
words, for Schweitzer, the centre of gravity had moved decisively
away from doctrines about the person of Jesus to the *vision* of
Jesus – the 'kingdom of God'. It is by becoming a fellow-worker
with Jesus, labouring with him in the purpose common to both,
that one comes to know him in a mysterious and inexpressible
way. Yet this 'strange-seeming' Jesus of the Gospels will always
remain alien to us, so remote was their world-view from the
modern world-view, or so Schweitzer believed.

There is a sense of loss in Schweitzer's writings – the Jesus
of history is no longer accessible to us – but also a sense of
liberation. For now we no longer have to define ourselves – or
others – by what articles of faith about Jesus are accepted or
denied. In *My Life and Thought* (1931) he wrote:

> Jesus does not require of men today that they be able to grasp
> either in speech or in thought Who He is. He did not think
> it necessary to give those who actually heard His sayings any
> insight into the secret of His personality, or to disclose to
> them the fact that He was that descendant of David who was
> one day to be revealed as the Messiah. The one thing He did
> require of them was that they should actively and passively
> prove themselves men who had been compelled by Him to
> rise from being as the world to being other than the world,
> and thereby partakers of His peace.

Thus, as Schweitzer puts it, 'the true understanding of Jesus
is the understanding of will acting on will'. Schweitzer had done
a year's military conscription in the German army, and the language of *command, will* and *obedience* may reflect his own
cultural background. Today I would express it more in terms
of leadership. Do we or do we not accept Jesus as a leader? Jesus
may have been wrong about the imminence of the 'kingdom of
God' on earth, but he bequeathed us a compelling vision. As,
inspired by the vision, we find our own place or vocation in the
service of the coming of the 'kingdom of God' on earth, so we
draw closer to Jesus. As Antoine de Saint-Exupéry said, *love*

*does not consist in gazing at each other but in looking together
in the same direction.* For Albert Schweitzer it is clear that the
living presence of the 'kingdom of God' as a compelling vision
was not imperilled by the 'false prophecy' of Jesus in the historical situation of his day. He could live with the error of Jesus.
For God, the ultimate Leader of humanity on its long journey
in time, was flexible: not all his pathways are known to us.
What matters above all is to co-operate with God by doing the
work for which we are called. Schweitzer again:

> We of today do not, like those who were able to hear the
> preaching of Jesus, expect to see a Kingdom of God realizing
> itself in supernatural events. Our conviction is that it can only
> come into existence by the power of the spirit of Jesus work-
> ing in our hearts and in the world. The one important thing
> is that we shall be as thoroughly dominated by the idea of
> the Kingdom, as Jesus required His followers to be.

It is as if we are being told that we can travel light on this
journey, like those first disciples who needed no extra clothes,
staffs, bags of food, purses or even shoes. The yoke of this Jesus
is both easy and also infinitely demanding.

Long before he wrote *The Quest of the Historical Jesus*,
Schweitzer had already decided on his own contribution to the
'kingdom of God'. In *My Life and Thought*, Schweitzer describes
how even as a schoolboy he was acutely aware and thinking
continually of the care and suffering encountered by others
around him, in contrast to his own happy childhood. Thankful-
ness and compassion for others became the mainspring of his
evolving sense of vocation:

> Then one brilliant summer morning at Günsbach, during the
> Whitsuntide holidays – it was in 1896 – there came to me,
> as I awoke, the thought that I must not accept this happiness
> as a matter of course, but must give something in return for
> it. Proceeding to think the matter out at once with calm
> deliberation, while the birds were singing outside, I settled
> with myself before I got up, that I would consider myself

justified in living till I was thirty for science and art, in order to devote myself from that time forward to the direct service of humanity. Many a time already I had tried to settle what meaning lay hidden for me in the saying of Jesus: 'Whosoever would save his life shall lose it, and whosoever shall lose his life for My sake and the Gospel's shall save it.' Now the answer was found. In addition to the outward, I now had inward happiness.

What would be the character of the activities thus planned for the future was not yet clear to me. I left it to circumstances to guide me. One thing only was certain, that it must be directly human service, however inconspicuous the sphere of it . . .

Schweitzer embarked upon a long quest for a suitable form of that service in Europe. It was not until six years after that morning at Günsbach, however, that an article in the magazine of the Paris Missionary Society entitled 'The Need of the Congo Mission' caught his eye. It appealed for doctors and nurses.

The writer expressed his hope that his appeal would bring some of those 'on whom the Master's eyes already rested' to a decision to offer themselves for this urgent work. The conclusion ran: 'Men and women who can reply simply to the Master's call, "Lord, I am coming," those are the people whom the Church needs.' The article finished, I quietly began my work. My search was over.

From Periphery to Centre

Having qualified as a doctor, Schweitzer worked for the rest of his life – interspersed with visits to Europe – at the hospital he built at Lambarene in French Equatorial Africa. It was direct compassionate service to individuals in need. It was the language of deeds, a service he could render without talking. In our own time we have seen a similar model of such compassionate service in the life and work of Mother Teresa for the destitute and dying in Calcutta, and eventually through the order of nuns she founded in many other cities.

Yet is service to the 'kingdom of God' to be done only upon the margins of society as it were, to the outcast, the sick, the elderly or the dying? Is there no vision for the centre of society, for those who are not to be found and cared for in its peripheral borders but stand at the very heart of it? What is the vision for the leaders of the world? Are they in fact leaders rather than rulers, leaders with a vision of tomorrow's world? Is there an overall direction for action in the interlocking political and social, economic and ecological spheres of life?

'Better fifty years of Europe than a cycle of Cathay', Tennyson the Poet Laureate of the Victorian age had written in his poem *Locksley Hall*. The thought in the line reflects the optimism and confidence in gradual, inevitable and unending progress which so gripped the imagination of his contemporaries and indeed inspired them:

> Not in vain the distance beacons. Forward, forward, let us range.
> Let the great world spin for ever down the ringing grooves of change.
> Thro' the shadow of the globe we sweep into the younger day:
> Better fifty years of Europe than a cycle of Cathay.

Yet in 1914 these leaders of progress, the European nations, went to war with each other and involved their empires in a conflict that cost some twenty million lives. Even Albert Schweitzer, living on the periphery of civilization in Africa, was caught up in the convulsion. Outside Günsbach, while walking on a road, his mother was killed by German cavalry horses. In 1917 he was shipped back to Europe with others to be interned for the duration of the war.

That year a young stretcher-bearer on the Western Front – a French Jesuit priest called Teilhard de Chardin – penned these thoughts in a letter to his cousin:

> You see, the more I think about it (as I've done a great deal during these recent marches) the more I feel the necessity of

defining and organizing the *total* natural effort. Individual
lives carry on from day to day; political foresight never goes
beyond short-term economic or territorial ambitions. . . .
Every one, every life, succeeds *at random*. Christianity indeed
contributes a common spirit and a common form; it makes
souls cleave together by charity. . . . But what positive, pro-
gressive, precise end are we to assign to human efforts? In
what natural direction are we to advance? To what tangible
end should we unite, all of us?

I can't believe that the world was given to man simply to
keep him busy, as if it were a wheel to turn. There must be
a precise effort to be made, a definite result to be obtained,
and this must be the *axis* of human world . . .

*The Making of a Mind: Letters of a Soldier Priest
1914–1919* (1965)

The stalemate and frustration of trench warfare was, as it were,
a parable for the stalled progress of humanity. New strategic
vision and new strategic thinking were called for to break the
deadlock and channel human energies in a new and fruitful
direction.

In that year of 1917, Russia withdrew from the war as a
consequence of the Communist overthrow of the Czarist monarchy. The principal author of Communism was Karl Marx and
behind the long and turgid tome he produced was the vision of
a utopia on earth which in some respects was not unlike a
secular version of the 'kingdom of God'.

Marx claimed to have established a science which could give
understanding of change in history, just as Darwin had suggested
the mechanism of change in the evolution of species, which he
called natural selection. Marx, however, believed in revolution
rather than evolution. Because the privileged classes would not
surrender power easily, the proletariat must rise, throw off their
chains and seize it from them. The iron laws of change in history
would assure them of victory. For power and economic might
always march together. The proletariat had the economic
muscle; therefore power would come to them – if they took it.
The 'Age of the Common Man' was about to dawn.

Thus, in the clothes of Communism, the Judaeo-Christian belief that history moves forwards in a line, not round in circles, was imported by Lenin into Russia and by Mao Tse-tung into China. Tennyson could not foresee that the philosophy of his contemporary Karl Marx would eventually change even the eastern mindset of Cathay (China).

The re-emergence of the 'kingdom of God' as a concept within the Christian churches can be roughly dated to the Second World War. In England, for example, Archbishop William Temple played a leading role in the Church of England's thinking about the social order. He saw the Christian church as an agent of the 'kingdom of God' for change in the political and social order. In *Citizen and Churchman* (1941), Temple wrote: 'In place of the Power-State we are led to that of the Welfare-State.' Although a Christian socialist in his own thinking, Temple did not make the error of identifying the 'kingdom of God' with any particular political theory. 'There is no structural organization of society which can bring about the coming of the Kingdom of God on earth,' he wrote, 'since all systems can be perverted by the selfishness of man.'

In *The Idea of a Christian Society* (1939), Temple's contemporary T. S. Eliot was also careful to underline that there was a tendency for

> speculation on a possible Christian order in the future to tend to come to rest in a kind of apocalyptic vision of a golden age of virtue ... But we have to remember the Kingdom of Christ on earth will never be realized, and that it always is being realized; we must remember that whatever reform or revolution we carry out, the result will always be a sordid travesty of what human society should be though the world is never left wholly without glory.

William Temple died in 1944 at the age of sixty-three, barely two years after becoming Archbishop of Canterbury. 'The Christian Church is the one organization in the world that exists purely for the benefit of non-members,' he wrote. One wonders what kind of inspired leadership Temple would have given to the Church of England in the post-war years. Would a man of such a vision of the church have succeeded in reorientating it to the 'kingdom of God' – a task which now seems impossible?

In the year of Temple's death a 39-year-old German Lutheran theologian and pastor, Dietrich Bonhoeffer, conceived it as his duty to the 'kingdom of God' to take part in a plot to assassinate Hitler. He was arrested and spent some months in prison before being hanged in Flossenburg concentration camp a week before the war ended. His *Letters and Papers from Prison*, published in 1953, reveal a radical mind at work, questioning for example the common assumption that Jesus had founded a religion. 'We are moving towards a completely religionless time,' he wrote; 'people as they are now simply cannot be religious any more.'

To be a Christian, Bonhoeffer believed, is to be called to share in the 'sufferings of God in the world'. For, he implied, it is as if God needs our help to bring about his 'kingdom', even to the extent of sharing in his sufferings to that end. 'God is weak and powerless in the world, and that is precisely the way, the only way, in which he is still with us and helps us. . . . Only the suffering of God can help.'

To work with God, then, is to share in his transforming love for this world, whatever the personal cost. 'It is only when one loves life and the earth so much that one may believe in the resurrection and the new world,' wrote Bonhoeffer, who incidentally was engaged to be married at the time. 'It may be that the day of judgment will dawn tomorrow; in that case, we shall gladly stop working for a better future. *But not before.*'

The New Nazarenes

What should we call those committed to working with Jesus for the 'kingdom of God' and yet who feel no need to give an opinion about who Jesus really was? I suggest 'the New Nazarenes' as a possible name. 'Nazarenes' predates 'Christians' as the name given to the disciples or companions of Jesus. I discuss the possible origin and meaning of the name in Note 1.

The original Nazarenes were certainly not as sophisticated in their theology as their successors the later Christians, who tended to dismiss them as spiritual Neanderthals. They spoke Aramaic as their first language and lived mostly in the Roman province of Syria which of course in those days included Galilee and Judaea. They had their own Aramaic or Hebrew version of Matthew's Gospel, though they varied only in unimportant details from the Greek text. The Nazarenes held that being a follower of Jesus and remaining a Jew were entirely compatible and made sense before the 'kingdom of God' was actually established on earth. Mainly for this reason they came to be regarded as heretics and eventually faded away. The Jews called them *Nazri*, and in Arabic today Christians are still known as *Nasarani*, a persistence of the Semitic form. By resurrecting their name, I am suggesting that today it is possible to be committed to actively seeking Jesus' vision of 'the kingdom of God on earth' and yet also be Muslim or Buddhist, Jew or Hindu, agnostic or atheist. Deep in the human heart is the belief that the vision of Jesus was simple, and that it is other later minds who have introduced the definitions and complications that largely divide us. It is as if the 'kingdom of God' is owned by none and has open frontiers: all are called to its service, from east and west, north and south.

To see the 'kingdom of God' in Bonhoeffer's words as a concept for a religionless world, to see it as something that transcends religion – always a source of division as well as strength among humankind – is to see its gates open wide. In the Revelation to John (21:1–2, 22) the seer saw a vision of 'a new heaven and earth; for the first heaven and the first earth had passed away, and the sea was no more. And I saw the holy city, new Jerusalem, coming down out of heaven from God . . . *And I saw no temple in the city*, for its temple is the Lord God . . .' To find the whole world holy, and all that is in it, would spell the end of religion as we have known it. In that vision all religions are striving to put themselves out of business.

The 'kingdom of God', as it were, 'comes down out of heaven'. No human or human institution invented the vision, nor does any philosophy, religion or church own it – we can make it our own only by living in its spirit. No one nation, creed or philosophy can claim it: it transcends church and synagogue,

mosque and temple. Yet, paradoxically, it gives us a true understanding of their function and purpose.

One church leader who believed passionately in the relevance
of Jesus' leadership vision for the world today was Cardinal
Basil Hume, Archbishop of Westminster. Speaking in 1991 to
a gathering of Catholic theologians in Britain on the theme that
a reborn Europe must seek lost vision and values, he was
reported in *The Times* as saying:

> The Church's mission is both universal and particular. There
> is a global responsibility as well as one which is national and
> continental. The concern for our immediate country and its
> neighbours must never for instance blind us to the needs of
> the Southern hemisphere. To the best of our ability we must
> keep alive in our continent the sense that solidarity, interde-
> pendence and practical concern embrace the whole planet.
>
> Europe is a community in search of identity, meaning and
> purpose. State Communism is being consigned shamefacedly
> to the scrap-heap. Liberal capitalism successfully meets many
> material needs but is extravagant in its use of irreplaceable
> resources and has little to say to the spirit of man. The peoples
> of Europe may well seek in religion and nationalism the
> answer to their deeper needs. But only a more spiritual, con-
> templative, truly renewed faith will save Europe's soul.
>
> The Kingdom of God needs to be maintained first and
> foremost in the lives of individuals. Here is the rich soil in
> which the seed of God's word is to be sown. But the seed
> will not take root and flourish until individuals, taking res-
> ponsibility for their own destiny, speak the truth and live the
> truth; unless they are vigilant in defence of their own liberty
> and that of others; unless they insist on justice for themselves
> and are scrupulously fair in dealing with others; unless they
> remain true to their deepest selves in all that they do. Society
> itself must reflect and foster those qualities and values.
>
> Our task is not so much to convince people of their sin-
> fulness but of their dignity and destiny as children of God,
> made in his image and called in Christ to make all things
> new. Nothing can totally disfigure that likeness or reduce the

need to approach each individual with absolute respect. Does this sound like Utopia, the perfect and painless society? It is rather the Kingdom of God, the civilization of love, to be built painfully, stone by living stone, out of human lives prepared to sacrifice all in the search for true life and lasting love. Do not tell them what to avoid; speak to them rather of what they can achieve. Give them ideals for which to strive: truth, freedom, justice, community. The European home we labour to build for all its people must enshrine these values.

Not that we can ever *define* what the 'kingdom of God' means. Jesus did not attempt to do so, and so we are hardly likely to succeed. But, it has been said, wherever the bounds of beauty, truth and goodness are advanced, there is the 'kingdom'. We discover its meaning as we respond to its calling and work for the realization of its values in society – universal and particular.

If you do not wish for His kingdom, don't pray for it. But if you do, you must do more than pray for it; you must work for it.

John Ruskin

10

On Humility

On a journey the lord of a people is their servant.
The prophet Muhammad

All too often in the Western tradition, leadership is associated with overpowering personalities possessed of a self-confidence that often turns into megalomania. As Lord Acton said, 'Power tends to corrupt, and absolute power corrupts absolutely.' In my own lifetime I have seen rulers such as Hitler, Mussolini and Stalin 'lording it' over their subjects as autocrats. All three of these despots could have waded in the blood of people shed directly or indirectly as a result of their wills. Such images caused a revulsion against the very idea of leadership – even today the word *Führer*, leader, is virtually unusable in the German language. Yet what is rejected here is *mis*leadership, not leadership. We know that real democracy cannot exist without good leaders – and leaders for good.

Egotism and arrogance are *not* integral to leadership but blemishes on its face. The seeds of a new awareness of the importance of humility as a leadership quality can be traced back to the Second World War. It is significant that the greatest of the Allied strategic leaders – Eisenhower, Alexander and Slim – were men of humility as well as men of integrity. They lacked any trace of arrogance, and that helped them to establish good relations with their 'co-workers', their allies. They held themselves accountable if things went wrong rather than blaming their subordinates or colleagues. As far as possible at their level of command, they shared the hardships and dangers of their soldiers. Paradoxical as it may seem, the humility these generals displayed had a functional value – it was one strand in their effectiveness as commander-in-chiefs of citizen armies composed of millions of free and equal men and women. Yet it was not until new light was shed on humility in leadership from an unlikely quarter – Japan – that the West sat up and took notice of a forgotten strand in its own tradition.

The Apostle of Humility – Lao Tzu

After the war Japanese industry was reconstituted with American help. The new Japanese managers revealed a far more self-effacing style of leadership than was common in the West. One influence that helped to shape the Japanese tradition in this respect had emanated from China in the fourth century BC – Taoism.

Lao Tzu was a native of Ch'u, a large state on the southern frontier. Almost nothing is known about him apart from what can be gleaned from the legends that surround his name. He probably served one of the ruling princes of China as a court sage and then he became a recluse in a hermitage. Even his book of sayings, entitled the *Tao Tê Ching*, has been much revised by later hands. So much so, in fact, that some scholars have doubted if Lao Tzu ever existed as an individual. In order to fill the gap of knowledge about Lao, events connected with various characters in Chinese mythology were ascribed to him at an early date.

After the resurrection of Jesus, the first followers of Jesus as the Messiah spoke of themselves as those in 'the Way' or 'the Way of God'. 'Way' is the literal meaning of *Tao* in Chinese. The 'Way' that Lao had in mind is not easy to define. It is really Nature's way: the order, course or pattern of all things created.

For the school of Chinese philosophers who thought as Master Lao, every person and thing is only what it is in relation to others. Events fall into harmony if left alone. Someone who intuitively understands this energy in Nature, and works intelligently with the grain of natural phenomena, is a follower of the *Tao*.

'The *Tao* principle is what happens of itself,' wrote Lao Tzu. The art of living, then, is more like steering a boat than struggling with an opponent. The image of water, flowing or still in cool, clear ponds, is never far from Lao's mind. *Tzu jan,*

'Nature', is that which is of itself. It is spontaneous. Everything grows and operates independently, on its own, but in harmony with all.

The principle of *wu wei*, the gentleness of not forcing things, is a natural corollary to this vision of the world. Working with the grain, rolling with the punch, swimming with the tide, trimming the sails to the wind, taking the tide at its flood: these are metaphors that reflect the spirit of *wu wei*.

If followers of the *Tao* understand the principles, structures or trends of human nature, human society and the natural order, then they can expend least energy in dealing with them. When they do exert their power at the right moment, then their efforts will have a spontaneous, natural or unforced quality about them.

Power or virtue is something within a person, and it is enhanced by following the *Tao*, or 'that from which nothing can deviate'. Chuang Tzu, a later member of the Taoist school of thought, expressed it thus: 'In an age of perfect virtue, good men are not appreciated; ability is not conspicuous. Rulers are mere beacons, while the people are as free as the wild deer. They love one another without being conscious of charity. They are true without being conscious of loyalty.'

On leadership, the following words of Lao Tzu have become justly famous:

> A leader is best,
> When people are hardly aware of his existence,
> Not so good when people praise his government,
> Less good when people stand in fear,
> Worst, when people are contemptuous.
> Fail to honour people, and they will fail to honour you.
> But of a good leader, who speaks little,
> When his task is accomplished, his work done,
> The people say, 'We did it ourselves!'

For Lao Tzu it is always some want within the inner life of the ruler that causes trouble among the people. If the leader lacks faith or trust, so will the people. The principle that 'there are no bad students but only bad teachers' is very much in keeping with the spirit of Taoist thought. So too is the military maxim that 'there are no bad soldiers, only bad officers'. These sayings invite leaders to look in the mirror before they find fault with others.

Humility in Action – Mahatma Gandhi

Speaking for myself, the Taoist tradition gives me a better understanding of the humility of Jesus and why humility characterizes the greatest leaders. Mahatma Gandhi was such a leader, and his life illustrated just how effective humility in leadership can be. *Mahatma* in Sanskrit means 'great soul' or 'great spirit'.

The fragile-looking man – a frail, barefooted man dressed in a *dhoti* of hand-spun cotton – advocated a simple, non-violent way of life. In 1932 he started a 'fast unto death' to demand rights for the lowest of the Indian castes – the 'Untouchables'. Later, in 1942, as a member of the Indian National Congress, Gandhi was arrested for his part in the campaign to remove India from the British empire. Home Rule was eventually granted in 1947. During the transfer of power from the British, Gandhi toured India trying to build peace between Hindu and Muslim. At the age of seventy-nine he fasted for five days to try to prevent war between them.

Such is the bare outline of Gandhi's story. Through his asceticism and his popularity with the masses of poorer Indians, born out of his complete identification with their lifestyle and aspirations, Gandhi acquired an immense influence. He was the only one among the top leaders who adopted the dress and lifestyle of the poor masses. As a political leader Gandhi was not especially great. His real greatness lies in his spiritual and moral leadership of India. His strength came from his closeness to the people.

An attractive warmth pervaded Gandhi's attitude to the Untouchables, those Indians so lowly that they had no place in even the lowest of the four main caste-groups that together made up the ladder of incarnation. Gandhi gave these Untouchables a name – *Harijans*, God's people. With a clear eye, he not only saw that the caste system was the key threat to India's unity and harmony, but he took what symbolic action he could to bring that message home. But he led by example. As Simone Weil wrote: 'He who treats as equals those who are far below him in strength really makes them a gift of the equality of human beings, of which fate had deprived them.'

People travelled miles to see Gandhi. In India, even looking upon a holy man from afar is believed to give the beholder a share in his *darshan* – his inner spiritual integrity or power. People wanted to touch Gandhi, too, in order to have contact with this integrity, just as the throngs reached out hands to Jesus in order to touch him. With Gandhi, as with Jesus, people touched his feet or the hem of his garment, for by doing so they gave a sign that they had humbled themselves as near to the ground as possible. Many who were friends or disciples of *Bapu* (father), or otherwise knew him well, still have about them the aura of this charming and friendly man, and embody the stoiç self-discipline he inspired.

At the heart of the Indian experience lay the concept of spiritual quest for truth, a seeking after a state of being which is higher than the present plane of existence. Because he so manifestly followed that way, Gandhi achieved his massive popularity. His life was a spiritual quest, he maintained, and political activity came from it as a secondary mode of expression. His emphasis on right and wrong in the moral sense, in what the secularized British held to be political matters, struck a deep chord in the Indian villages. For the Indian villager also saw life in the context of an eternal struggle between good and evil.

Gandhi's quest for spiritual truth in religions other than his own, notably in the Gospels, was entirely in keeping with the eclectic tradition of Hinduism and also the primacy of the spiritual search for truth. But his search for a universal God, transcending the religions and sects of the world, also had political implications. Both before and after Independence, the most pressing issue for India was the division between those of the Hindu and Muslim faiths. Gandhi's search for a common God might have provided a source of unity, for in drawing near to God people draw near to each other. It was the instinct of a New Nazarene.

Above all, Gandhi wanted to see India preserved as a unity.

If bloodshed was inevitable, let it be within India rather than between divided nations on the sub-continent. Gandhi's critics may well be right in their charge that in this respect he was naïve and unrealistic. Gandhi is also open to the criticism that he did not attempt to win over the Muslim leader, Muhammad Ali Jinnah, to his vision of India before his attitude had hardened beyond change. By the time Gandhi bestirred himself, the British, under Mountbatten's camouflage screen of charm, were beginning to wash their hands of India. Partition gave them a face-saving exit from the sub-continent.

On 30 January 1948, Gandhi was in Delhi at the house where his evening prayer meetings were held, and was several minutes late for the meeting. As he approached the waiting crowd with his grand-nieces, a young man greeted him from a few feet away with the customary Hindu salutation of folded hands. Gandhi smiled at him and, according to one version, spoke to him. The young man, a Hindu Brahmin fanatic, then whipped out a pistol and fired three times at point-blank range. The bullets lodged in Gandhi's chest, stomach and groin. Gandhi raised his hands above his hand in the same salutation, fell down and died minutes later.

Nobility in Leadership – Nelson Mandela

Nelson Mandela has shown the world a lofty and courageous spirit, a nobility of feeling and generosity of mind. Such a spirit enables a leader to bear trouble calmly, to disdain meanness and revenge, and to make sacrifices for worthy ends. It can also enter the mood of a nation.

The man who has become such an inspirational figure was born in 1918, the eldest son of a Xhosa chief (the Xhosas are the next biggest tribe to the Zulus) in what is now the nominally independent homeland called Transkei. After training as a lawyer, he joined the African National Congress in 1944 and was a leader of the Congress's non-violent campaigns against apartheid during the 1950s.

After police killed sixty-nine unarmed black protesters at Sharpeville in 1960, Mandela and other Congress leaders began

to abandon their hopes for peaceful change. In 1961 they formed
the Congress's military wing, *Umkhonto we Sizwe* (The Spear
of the Nation).

Mandela evaded arrest, earning the nickname 'The Black Pim-
pernel', until August 1962, when he was jailed for five years for
incitement and leaving the country illegally. In 1963 he was
tried again, along with other underground leaders, and in 1964
was jailed for life for sabotage, which he openly admitted. At
his trial, Mandela spoke of 'the ideal of a democratic and free
society in which all persons live together in harmony and with
equal opportunities. It is an ideal which I hope to live for and
to achieve, but if need be an ideal for which I am prepared to
die.'

As Mandela began his long sojourn in the harsh outpost of
the South African prison system, Robben Island, he resolved
that he would not allow this experience to remove from him his
essential dignity as a person:

> In and of itself, that assured that I would survive, for any
> man or institution that tries to rob me of my dignity will lose
> because I will not part with it at any price or under any
> pressure. I never seriously considered the possibility that I
> would not emerge from prison one day. I never thought that
> a life sentence truly meant life and that I would die behind
> bars. Perhaps I was denying this prospect because it was too
> unpleasant to contemplate. But I always knew that someday
> I would once again feel the grass under my feet and walk in
> the sunshine as a free man.

James Gregory, Mandela's jailer for twenty years, has written
a book about his prisoner who became a friend. Soon after his
arrival he had his first dramatic encounter with Mandela, then
working in slave labour conditions in the searing light and heat
of the Robben Island lime quarry, scene of many a fearful atroc-
ity. Prisoners were beaten and abused and had dogs set on them.
It was here that Gregory saw Mandela, standing tall, 'his ramrod
back and broad shoulders prominent' in his prison shorts and
sandals, amidst a group of prisoners, his whole body, says

Gregory, a statement that 'I am a leader. You will not intimidate me.' Mandela greeted Gregory with a firm good morning and 'Welcome to Robben Island' and Gregory, before he knew it, slipped into the Zulu greeting he had not used since childhood, a mark of respect which left Mandela stunned.

Gradually the two men became friends. When Mandela's son Thembi was killed in a road traffic accident, Gregory, then a young man, lent him what support he could. At exactly the same age although almost twenty years later, Gregory's son was killed in a car crash, and Mandela appears to have saved Gregory from despair and even suicide by talking to him daily for weeks. Saying farewell to this prison warden whom he had known for twenty-three years, Mandela embraced him with tears in his eyes. 'The wonderful hours we spent together during the last two decades end together,' he wrote in a note, 'but you will always be with me in my thoughts.'

After his release from prison – 'these long, lonely, wasted years' as he wrote – Mandela showed the rare quality of *magnanimity*, which from the Latin means literally *greatness of spirit*. For the Greeks and Romans it was the sure sign of a great leader. Stemming from a well-founded high regard for oneself, *magnanimity* manifests itself as generosity of spirit and equanimity in the face of trouble or adversity.

A magnanimous leader such as Nelson Mandela lacks any kind of pettiness and rises above even justified resentment. Consider what he endured. His children were traumatically affected by those years, his first wife Evelyn was unprepared to accept his allegiance to the ANC, he was unable to pay his last respects to his mother or his son. Add to that the government's relentless persecution of his family. He says: 'To see your family, your children, being persecuted when you are absolutely helpless in jail, that is one of the most painful experiences I have had. . . . Your wife being hounded from job to job, your children being taken out of Coloured schools, police breaking into your house at midnight and even assaulting your wife.'

Yet not once does he express bitterness towards the white community for his grim ordeal, only against the system they imposed. How typical that upon his release from prison, he called for the blacks to exhibit generosity of spirit; and on the day of South Africa's first free election (27 April 1994) he spoke of the need to give the white minority 'confidence and security'.

Even when Mandela met Percy Yutar, the lawyer who had led the prosecution in the trial that ended with his sentence to prison all those years ago, he smiled and placed his arm around the slender shoulders of his one-time adversary, now eighty-four years old, saying what had happened was now truly in the past. After this meeting, Percy Yutar described the President as a 'saintly man'. And Mandela invited his jailer James Gregory and his family as guests of honour to his presidential inauguration. His natural authority and charisma are evident to all those who meet him, and he possesses the gift of a winning smile. He remains courteous and attentive to individuals, whatever their age or status. He retains the common touch, greeting workers and heads of state with the same warm civility and punctilious manners.

It is such generosity of spirit that makes Nelson Mandela one of the world's most significant moral leaders since Gandhi. His moral stature stands out even more in an age so often deprived of political morality. His greatest achievement has been to create, through nobility in leadership, a climate in which the new South Africa could collect itself for the journey that lies ahead.

Yet more than anything else, it is Nelson Mandela's self-sacrifice that has set him apart. No other leader in modern times has so clearly shown that the spirit and principles exemplified by Jesus really do work. Even the love of one's enemy is shown to be a form of practical wisdom. To make peace with an enemy, one must work with an enemy until that enemy becomes your partner, he wrote in his autobiography *Long Walk to Freedom*.

Shortly after his election as President of South Africa, Nelson Mandela issued a message which reflected the spirit of a humble man. After a tribute to his partner in the ending of apartheid Mandela points to the greatness that is in the people of South Africa:

I would like to take this opportunity to thank the world leaders who have given messages of support. I would also congratulate Mr F. W. De Klerk for the four years that we have worked together, quarrelled, addressed sensitive problems and at the end of our heated exchanges were able to shake hands and to drink coffee.

To the people of South Africa and the world who are watching, the election has been a triumph for the human spirit.

South Africa's heroes are legends across the generations. But it is the people who are our true heroes. The election victory is one of the most important moments in the life of South Africa. I am proud of the ordinary, humble people of South Africa who have shown such a calm, patient determination to reclaim South Africa, and joy that we can loudly proclaim from the rooftops – free at last!

I intend to be a servant not a leader, as one above others. I pledge to use all my strength and ability to live up to the world's expectation of me.

With his immense moral authority gained by the patient and magnanimous bearing of adversity, Mandela shows us that it is possible to be a servant first and then a leader, one who serves by leading and leads to serve. The old mould of leadership which simply set one up above others is broken for ever. Free at last!

After his release from twenty-seven years in prison Mandela experienced a personal loneliness after the brutal, public break-up of his second marriage. 'I am the loneliest man,' he said. His third marriage, to Graça Machel, widow of the ruler of Mozambique, changed the picture. 'I am blooming because of the love and support she has given me,' he said. 'She is the boss. When I am alone I am very weak.' Of Madiba – Mandela's clan name, meaning 'revered one' – Graça said recently:

People say my husband is a saint, but I don't know about that. I am probably one of the few people who know him best outside politics, and to me he is just a human being who is simple and gentle. At the same time so generous and keen to give love and so eager to receive it. That is what matters to me and that's what unites us.

Vision, humility and vulnerability: these are the hallmarks of the leadership exemplified by Jesus and seen today in such new Nazarenes as Mahatma Gandhi and Nelson Mandela. These are the characteristics, along with professional competence or ability, that free and equal people will look for in leaders in every field of endeavour. All leaders now need these qualities.

One other New Nazarene in modern times – no stranger, too, to bitter personal loneliness – was Dag Hammarskjöld. Son of a Swedish prime minister, he became the world's leading civil servant as Secretary-General of the United Nations in 1953 and held that job until his death in a plane crash in 1958 while on his way to attempt a peaceful settlement in the war-torn Congo. After his death a book of his reflections was published under the title of *Markings*. That word translates the Swedish phrase *Väg märken*, which means the waymarks or stone cairns that are found beside mountain paths. One of Dag Hammarskjöld's 'markings' concerns the humility needed for those in positions of power, and it has a universal relevance. As he sat alone in his room one night Hammarskjöld reminded himself:

Your position never gives you the right to command. It only imposes on you the duty of so living your life that others can receive your orders without being humiliated.

11

On Leadership – Timeless and Timely

But of a good leader, who speaks little,
When their task is accomplished, their work done,
The people say, 'We did it ourselves.'

after Lao Tzu

If we are to progress, this world needs leadership – at all levels, in all lands and in every field of human endeavour. But the new millennium calls for a new and more global kind of leadership, one that respects our essential humanity and the dignity of each individual. It is not to be confused with holding positions of so-called power or possessing great wealth or having high status in society. As the challenges ahead of us become more severe, more will be expected from those who are called to positions of leadership responsibility. What light does the example and teaching of Jesus throw upon this 'still more excellent way' that leaders in all walks of life must now tread?

It is impossible to answer that question in one book, let alone one chapter. All that I can do by way of conclusion is to offer you some personal reflections concerning the differences that Jesus' example as a leader and his teachings have made to my own search for understanding about leadership.

That quest began a long time ago when I was still a schoolboy at St Paul's School in London. A leader of Renaissance scholarship in England, John Colet, the Dean of St Paul's, had founded it in 1509 with the help of his friend Erasmus. Their vision was of a Christian school that would produce 'citizens of the world'. So they set the number of boys at 153 – the number of fish in the miraculous draught – and opened it to 'the children of all nations'. It was the first school in England to teach Greek, the language of Socrates and Xenophon. Over the centuries it proved to be a nursery of leaders in many fields – Milton,

Marlborough, Montgomery. To the school historical society, I spoke on the subject of 'Leadership in History'. The school magazine carried this brief report:

> Leadership, he said, could be defined as the activity of influencing people to pursue a certain course; there must also be some power of mind behind the leader. Leadership is not merely the authority of the commander, but contains by necessity some strange strength of personality which attracts the ordinary man. It is only when the times are favourable that a man of destiny can come into his own. Although leadership may change in this aspect from age to age, the qualities of a leader are the same.

Many years later, having devoted much of my professional life to leadership and leadership development, I find that this summary is not far off the mark in reflecting what I think today. Sometimes first thoughts are best.

Is Charisma Necessary?

'Some strange strength of personality' . . . since those days that has been labelled *charisma*. *Webster's Dictionary* defines it as: '[Greek, *charisma*, favour, gift, from *charizesthai* to favour, from *charis* grace; akin to *charein* to rejoice] (1) an extraordinary power (as of healing) given a Christian by the Holy Spirit for the good of the church; (2) *a personal magic of leadership arousing special popular loyalty or enthusiasm for a statesman or military commander.*' Is charisma in this second sense – 'personal magic' – essential for leaders? Nelson certainly had it, and so perhaps did Jesus. But do we need it today in order to inspire others?

One morning, at London's Heathrow Airport, I glimpsed Mother Teresa bustling by, a diminutive figure with brown wrinkled face like a walnut and white veil edged with blue. She was accompanied by twelve or fifteen white-robed nuns swirling around her, like ducklings around their mother. At eighty-six, suffering from heart disease, Mother Teresa was still leading from the front. With 568 homes for the destitute and dying in

120 countries, she now had her sights on China. 'I have plenty of work to do, and I will be here until my last breath,' she told some waiting reporter. 'We have to pull on. We will continue God's work.' The following week I read that she handed over the reins of her Missionaries of Charity Order to her elected successor, Sister Nirmala.

At the public announcement of her successor's appointment, Mother Teresa intervened when Sister Nirmala, a 63-year-old Indian nun, was asked if she would be able to fill her charismatic predecessor's shoes. 'It doesn't matter if an individual has charisma. It all depends on God's will,' Mother Teresa said.

In this case 'God's will' was established by an eight-week process of selection, involving prayer and discussion by the 120 nuns qualified to vote. Doubtless they chose Sister Nirmala because she had the knowledge and experience, the personal qualities and natural ability needed in a leader. Both Indian and foreign volunteers hailed her as the best choice. She had, too, the gift of humility. Asked if she felt like the mission's leader, Sister Nirmala said: 'Mother is our foundress and we are all her children. I am not the head of the order. We are all equal.'

As we have seen, when Paul lists leadership among the gifts given to the church (1 Corinthians 12:27–31) the Greek word he uses – *kybernetes*, steersman or leader – is a *person*, not a 'personal magic' of the personality, like charm. Steersmanship called for technical mastery of the mariner's arts as well as the ability to win the willing and enthusiastic co-operation of the crew. When the great ship of Alexandria with 276 people on board taking him and his guards to Rome ran into violent storms, Paul himself showed the kind of calm, encouraging and inspiring leadership in a life-threatening crisis that is expected in a ship's captain (Acts 27).

To be helmsman and captain or leader on board a ship calls for more than professional and social skills, more even than the character and resourcefulness to cope with the unforeseen. The best master-mariners have a selfless attitude to the ship and the company who sail in it. Joseph Conrad, one himself, wrote in *The Mirror of the Sea*:

The genuine masters of their craft – I say this confidently from my experience of ships – have thought of nothing but of doing their best by the vessel under their charge. To forget one's self, to surrender all personal feelings in the service of that fine art, is the only way for a seaman to the faithful discharge of his trust.

If the ship sinks, such a captain is the last to leave it. Like the 'good shepherd' of whom Jesus spoke, he is willing to lay down his own life for the safety of the passengers and crew who have put their trust in him. It is leadership in this whole sense that makes it a gift for those fortunate enough to experience it.

What Paul has to say to us about charisma in our modern usage – the 'personal magic of leadership' – comes a few sentences later in his letter to the Corinthians, where he speaks of the gifts of faith, hope and love, which he expects to find in all who exercise any function in the church. Certainly it is difficult to think of any good leaders inside or outside the church who are devoid of faith and trust – in others as well as themselves – or hope. What oxygen is to the lungs, so hope is to the human spirit. The faith of Abraham is our model here: 'In hope he believed against hope' (Romans 4:18).

Love informs all relations, roles and functions, not just leadership. But where it is present in a leader it breeds not only patience and kindness – the gentleness of Jesus – but also humility:

> Love is not jealous or boastful; it is not arrogant or rude. Love does not insist on its own way; it is not irritable or resentful; it does not rejoice at wrong, but rejoices in the right. Love bears all things, believes all things, hopes all things, endures all things. (1 Corinthians 13:4–7)

If leadership includes a set of prosaic functions that have to be learned and mastered until they become skills, love is the salt which brings out its full colours and flavours. As Thomas Aquinas wrote, 'Grace does not destroy nature, it perfects it.'

Learning to Lead

In this book I have been at pains to stress what might be called the natural qualifications and abilities of Jesus, the attributes that made him the right man in the right place at the right time. In doing so I have run counter to the Gospels in the main, for they are intent upon stressing that his authority and command of others was supernatural, not something he could have acquired or learnt. When, for example, Jesus taught in the Temple, we are told that 'the Jews marvelled at it, saying, "How is it that this man has learning, when he has never studied?"' (John 7:15).

Certainly the authority with which Jesus spoke impressed itself on everyone who heard him, whether or not they agreed with what he said. 'And when Jesus finished these sayings, the crowds were astonished at his teaching, for he taught them as one who had authority, and not as their scribes' (Matthew 7:28–9). And again, as the Temple guards said to their masters on another occasion, 'No man ever spoke like this man!' (John 7:46).

According to Luke's Gospel this knowledge was always there. He has that charming story of Jesus, aged twelve, in the Temple's rabbinic school 'sitting among the teachers, listening to them and asking them questions; and all who heard him were amazed at his understanding and his answers' (Luke 2:46–7). Yet Josephus, destined by his birth for the priesthood, was also educated in the Temple, where, he tells us, by the age of about fourteen (*c.* AD 41) he had become such an authority on the intricacies of the Jewish Law that even the high priests and lay rulers in Jerusalem came to him for the elucidation of knotty problems. Legends do gather around great leaders, emphasizing their extraordinary powers, and it is sometimes difficult to distinguish fact from fiction.

Jesus not only acquired a great and ready knowledge of the scriptures – he must have had a retentive memory – but he also had the self-confidence to think for himself. To be able to simplify the highly complex Law of Moses to that integrated principle – 'You shall love the Lord your God and your neighbour'

– called at the time for highly unusual powers of analysis and creative synthesis, simple as the formula may seem to us. The fact that it came from Jesus spontaneously in response to a scribe's question, suggests that much of his creative thought was done unconsciously, as is so often the case with creative thinking. Inspiration's workshop lies somewhere in this subterranean realm.

But the knowledge that equipped him to lead was more comprehensive than knowing the scriptures or understanding the character of the 'kingdom of God', just as a steersman-leader must know more than how to read charts or how to navigate by the stars. There are signs, for example, that Jesus had learnt at least some of the extra knowledge required, such as the techniques used in faith-healing. Certainly, he had acquired some tricks of oratory, such as using in his parables memorable 'sets-of-three', such as, for example, three kinds of seed sown or three servants entrusted with talents. More substantially, Jesus had also evidently acquired the art of leadership by observation, reflection and experience. That reflective learning may have taken place, for instance, by naturally observing how good shepherds conducted their flocks or by noting how and why the rulers of his day had lost the hearts of their people – 'knowledge of good bought dear by knowing ill', as John Keats would later call it. But, as set out in Part One, there were also positive models or examples of good leadership available to him within the biblical tradition. Great as his natural genius for leadership may have been, Jesus was humble in his willingness to learn to lead, and therein lies his example for us today.

The Need for Humility

In the summer of 1952 Field Marshal Montgomery and Winston Churchill went for a walk together on the hill beside Chequers, the country residence of British prime ministers. Montgomery pressed Churchill to define a great man. Was Hitler great? No, replied Churchill, he made too many mistakes. But how, asked Montgomery, could Churchill maintain that Napoleon was great when he was the Hitler of the nineteenth century? And

surely the great religious leaders were the real great men? The
Prime Minister said their greatness was indisputable but it was
of a different kind. Christ's story was unequalled and his death
to save sinners unsurpassed; moreover the Sermon on the Mount
was the last word in ethics.

If we allow ourselves to think of the leadership of Jesus too
far along these lines as being of 'a different kind', it makes Jesus
so remote that we cannot learn from him. Most at risk in this
respect are those who for theological reasons see Jesus as a
perfect man in every respect, without a fault or blemish. Given
that assumption, by deduction he must have had *all* the qualities
that we associate with leadership, and at full strength. A book
about the leadership of Jesus would be a portrait of ideal leadership, such as Xenophon attempted in his study of Cyrus the
Great.

It is true that we can discern or legitimately infer in Jesus the
chief qualities we associate with leaders, even if, given the nature
of the available historical records they are in trace only: enthusiasm, integrity, vision, the balance of a demanding toughness and
fairness, the capacity for justified anger, calmness and coolness,
tenacity, warmth and humanity, courtesy and tact and – by no
means least – courage. For the situation in which Jesus found
himself demanded plenty of courage – after the death of John
the Baptizer, he was a marked man. Courage, of course, does
not imply the lack of fear, but the capacity to overcome it and
venture on. Yet it is when, in the traditional interpretation of
Gethsemane, Jesus seems to be wrestling with fear that we feel
closest to him.

Perhaps one of the greatest leaders in American history was
Franklin D. Roosevelt. Gripped by the Depression, the nation
thrilled to hear Roosevelt declare in his first Inaugural Address
(4 March 1933): 'Let me assert my firm belief that the only thing
we have to fear is fear itself.' Roosevelt's whole demeanour, and
that clear vibrant voice, heralded a leader at the helm. Yet in a
conversation with his son that evening by the fireside in the
White House, Roosevelt confessed that he was deeply afraid of
failure and prayed to God for help. 'Will you pray with me
tonight?' he asked his son. A leader with humility.

The fact that Jesus might be seen as having made errors and mistakes as a leader – not everything he did or said was right – should encourage all those who seek to lead in the timeless and timely way he pioneered. Humility embraces both the acceptance that however well-intentioned, we will make errors of judgment, and also the readiness to learn from them when they become obvious or are pointed out to us.

The Supreme Test

In the early afternoon of 14 February 1942, the British ship *SS Vyner Brook* was carrying some of the last civilians to escape before the capitulation of Singapore. Among the passengers were sixty-five nursing sisters from the Australian Army Nursing Service, distinct in their grey dresses, white cuffs and Red Cross armbands.

As the ship sailed through the treacherous strait between Sumatra and Bangka, it was attacked by Japanese bombers and quickly sank. It took eight hours for the survivors to reach Bangka by lifeboat where locals informed them the island was under Japanese control. During the night another British ship was shelled at sea and the survivors of the *SS Vyner Brook* were joined by the lifeboat bearing twenty English soldiers.

Injured, without food, and with no chance of escape, the party agreed to give themselves up to the occupiers. A handful of men went in search of the Japanese while the civilian women walked in another direction. Of the original 65 nurses, 22 had landed together and they remained on the beach, tending to the injured, along with the servicemen. When the Japanese arrived, the survivors were separated into men and women and the men were marched along the beach and round a headland. Shortly afterwards shots were heard. Then the Japanese soldiers returned alone, and sat in front of the women cleaning blood from their bayonets.

During the early afternoon, an officer instructed the nurses to walk from the palm-fringed Radjik Beach into the sea until they were waist deep in the waves. Fully aware of their fate, the nurses put on a brave face. Their matron, Irene Drummond, called out: 'Chin up, girls. I'm proud of you and I love you all.' At that point the Japanese fired.

By chance one nurse, Vivian Bullwinkel, shot through the groin, survived the massacre and it is to her that we owe this remarkable insight into true greatness as a leader. It reminds me of Jesus hanging in agony on the cross and yet speaking a word of hope and encouragement to his crucified and dying neighbour. Here is the ultimate test of leadership, to encourage and support others in the face of certain death, where there is no reward or advantage remaining except the love of those entrusted to one's care. The story throws a light back on the nature of good leadership in all the lesser passages of life. There can be no real love without a willingness to sacrifice. Do you love those with whom you are privileged to serve and to lead? If you do, then you will be prepared to sacrifice for them, if your responsibilities or the situation demand. You may have no choice, as in this case, but even the most negative can be turned into the positive, defeat into victory, death into life.

'He who would be a leader, should make himself a bridge', says an old Welsh proverb. It comes from a collection of ancient myths called *The Mabinogion*. In one a legendary Irish king called Bendigeidfran came with his army to a fabulous river. 'Lord,' said his noblemen, 'you know the peculiarity of this river: none can go through it, nor is there any bridge over it. What shall we do?' The king replied: 'There is no bridge, save that he who is a chief, let him be a bridge. I will myself be a bridge.' And then, after he had laid himself down across the river, hurdles were placed on him and his hosts passed through over him.

Towards Undiscovered Ends

We get to know people best when we are living and working alongside them. It is those who share in some limited measure the vision of Jesus and give themselves like him to doing 'God's work' in this world who catch the occasional glimpses of him in others.

'God's work', as we conceive it today, encompasses the

proper management of this world in so far as it is in our power to do so. Paul had once envisaged creation as 'groaning and travailing' as if it were struggling to share in the new-created order of the 'kingdom of God'. And that all-embracing vision was foreshadowed in Isaiah's prophecy of a time when a new harmony in nature would prevail: 'The wolf shall dwell with the lamb, and the leopard shall lie down with the kid ... for the earth shall be full of the knowledge of the Lord as the waters cover the sea' (11:6–10).

That sense of oneness or fellow-feeling with all creatures breeds compassion. There is a legend about the childhood of the Buddha, 'the Enlightened One', who was born Gautama (c. 563–483 BC), the son of a king of the Sáykyas, a tribe settled in northern India, and brought up in secluded luxury, isolated from the world.

> At the age of seven the Prince began his lessons in the civil and military arts, but his thoughts more naturally tended to other things. One spring day he went out of the castle with his father. Together they were watching a farmer at his ploughing when he noticed a bird descend to the ground and carry out a small worm which had been turned up by the farmer's plough. He sat down in the shade of a tree and thought about it, whispering to himself:
>
> 'Alas! Do all living creatures kill each other?'
>
> The Prince, who had lost his mother so soon after his birth, was deeply affected by the tragedy of these little creatures.
>
> This spiritual wound deepened day by day as he grew up; like a little scar on a young tree, the suffering of human life became more and more deeply ingrained in his mind.

The problem of suffering obsessed Gautama, and at the age of twenty-nine he left home and began a lifelong quest for its remedy. Compassion for his fellow humans led him to devote his life to finding ways they could evade this inexorable law of suffering through meditation and self-discipline. And his compassion for that worm writhing in the bird's beak – for all living creatures – is Buddha's enduring contribution to the 'kingdom of God'. It is echoed in the lives of Christian saints such as Anthony, Cuthbert and Francis of Assisi and all those today who work for the welfare of all that lives.

The concept of the 'kingdom of God', with its root in a long-disappeared Semitic world-view, will not ring bells for everyone. But, as Teilhard de Chardin discerned, humanity does need some stars to steer by, an axis of advance. It is as if the vanguard of humanity is groping its way forwards in the dark. The human enterprise is full of uncertainty and risk, but that is what makes it so attractive to us. Something completely prede-termined would cease to have any interest or challenge, it would be devoid of any moral significance for us.

The idea that God has given humankind something resem-bling a transcendent task, and that it draws together in so far as it works together as a team and makes progress, is worthy of reflection. It takes us back to the core idea that lies behind the story of Jesus, the idea of God himself as the Leader of humanity on its journey to 'undiscovered ends'. It is those who give most to that task who are the greatest among us. 'Man becomes great exactly in the degree in which he works for the welfare of his fellow-men,' said Mahatma Gandhi. On this axis, as Paul writes, those who work have the assurance that 'your labour is not in vain' (1 Corinthians 15:58).

'The task of leadership is not to put greatness into people, but to elicit it,' said John Buchan, 'for the greatness is there already.' Jesus and his vision are one of the greatest catalysts of all time for drawing out the hidden greatness in humanity. For those who aspire to that 'still more excellent way' of leadership he pioneered, Jesus is a perennial source of inspiration. If this book has achieved nothing else, I hope that it will be a signpost to that well and evidence that it will never run dry. One who loves, inspires us to love.

Notes

Note 1: The 'Nazarene'

'Nazarene' is a descriptive term applied to Jesus in the Gospels and his followers in Acts. The received explanation of this sobriquet is that Jesus came from a town called Nazareth. Second, it is assumed that Nazarenes – the first widely known name for his followers – derives in turn from the town name. The same epithet is also regularly applied in the Talmud to Jesus and his disciples. As the Synoptic Gospels were compiled from earlier source materials in the second half of the first century, it is hard to question a fact that has their authority and seems to be credible. But there may be another explanation.

In the Greek New Testament, two words correspond to 'Nazarene': *Nazarenos* and *Nazoraios*. The former occurs in four places in Mark, also in Luke 4:34 (where it may be dependent on the Marcan source). It occurs again in Luke 24:19, where, however, the reading is doubtful. In Matthew, John and Acts (and perhaps originally in Luke), *Nazoraios* is exclusively used.

Nazarenos (and presumably *Nazoraios*) looks as if it is derived from *Nazara* – like *Magdalene* from *Magdala* or *Gadarene* from *Gadara*. *Nazoraios* may be a dialect version of *Nazarenos*, but it is more likely that *Nazarenos* is simply the more Greek-sounding form of the word. It is thought by scholars that the *-et* and *-eth* endings of place names are Galilean dialect, so the name of the alleged place of origin in Hebrew/Aramaic may be rendered *Nazar* or *Nazara*. I say that because at this level of etymology we are really looking at a typical Semitic root in Hebrew/Aramaic of three consonants with uncertain vowel sounds: *nsr*.

In Matthew 2:23 it is stated that the child Jesus was brought to Nazareth that 'what was spoken by the prophets might be fulfilled, "He shall be called a Nazarene" (*Nazoraios* with no pronoun). The Semitic original of the word is probably *Nazara*, so it reads 'that he should be called *Nazara*'. The earliest extant version of Matthew in Hebrew actually has: 'for he shall be called *Nazareth*' (H. J. Schonfield, *An Old Hebrew Text of St Matthew's Gospel*, 1927). The Syriac version has *Nasraya*. What did *nsr* or *Nazara* mean?

There are in fact three possibilities: (1) it had a symbolic meaning; (2) it derived from a sect; and (3) the traditional place reference. Here I can do no more than briefly indicate the arguments and leave you to come to your own conclusion.

(1) Symbolic

There appears to be no prophecy in the Old Testament that matches Matthew 2:23. What did Matthew have in mind? Quite possibly Isaiah 11:1:

> There shall come forth a shoot from the stump of Jesse,
> and a branch shall grow out of his roots.
> And the Spirit of the Lord shall rest upon him . . .

Jesse was the father of David and the context is one of messianic expectation. The Hebrew Aramaic for 'shoot' or 'branch' is *nsr* or *neser*. The vowel sounds are uncertain, and the letter *tsade* in Hebrew (pronounced as in 'czar') had no equivalent in Greek and so is rendered as s or z. So *neser* could be *nazar* or *nazara*. This image of a *nazar*, a 'shoot' – a tree cut down and sprouting new growth from the stump – would serve as a symbol of the hopes for the restoration of the House of David after the last ruler was carried off into exile in Babylon in 586 BC (cf. Jeremiah 23:5, 33:15; Isaiah 4:2; Zechariah 3:8; 6:12). Such a restoration never occurred, but the Davidic prophecies were enormously influential in the New Testament.

If 'Nazarene' derived from this symbolic title the Gentile, Greek-speaking disciples in Antioch would have found it too Semitic, too hard to explain. So they substituted the Greek equivalent derived from *Chrestos* for the Aramaic *Nazara* (itself an obscure equivalent to the Hebrew *Messiah*, the anointed one). Hence 'Christian'.

The only relatively early supporter of this view is Epiphanius, and it is easy for traditionalists to dismiss him as late and unreliable. Epiphanius was born in Judaea about AD 310 and he spoke Aramaic as a native language. He became Bishop of Salamis, the main port of Cyprus, where Paul and Barnabas had once preached in the synagogue.

Although Epiphanius accepted the place-name derivation of 'Nazarene', he also tells us that the followers of Jesus were first called *Jessaians*. He acknowledged that this name *could* come from the name *Jesus*, but he clearly believed it came from *Jesse*, and thus stems from Isaiah 11:1, proof that the first followers of Jesus applied that prophecy to him.

There is another piece of evidence that the 'root' (*nazar*) image was applied to Jesus in the first century. The 'root' or 'shoot' image belongs to a wider metaphor of the ruler as a tree in the ancient Near East. One of the functions of kingship was to provide justice for the people; protection not only from those outside the community, but inside. The shelter-providing tree is a natural image of protection (cf. Daniel 4; Judges 9; Ezekiel 31). In the *Didache* (*c.* AD 95) occurs the phrase 'the Holy Vine of your son David'. In the Revelation of John (22:16) the author makes Jesus declare: 'I Jesus have sent my angel to you with this testimony for the churches. I am the root and the off-spring of David, the bright morning star.'

Although Paul makes no mention of Nazareth he did know that Jesus was 'descended from David according to the flesh' (Romans 1:3). It looks as if the physical descent of Jesus from David was an article of belief before the Gospels were written.

(2) Sect

The second possibility is that 'Nazarene' could refer to membership of a sect, like 'Essene'. The difficulty here is that – apart from Epiphanius – there is no evidence that such a sect existed.

The possibility that Jesus was a Nazirite (from the root *nzr*) can be dismissed. In the Old Testament, Nazirites were ascetics who had taken a vow, or whose parents had taken a vow on their behalf, as with Samuel and Samson. It is linked with the Arabic *nadara*, to make a vow. While Jesus was not a Nazirite as such, the root is associated with the more general idea of holiness in the Greek Septuagint. Some Christian writers, such as Eusebius and Tertullian, interpreted Matthew 2:23 in this way.

Epiphanius does mention a pre-Christian sect which he calls *Nasaraioi* or *Nasarenoi*, distinct from the later Christian sect (variously named by him as *Nazoraioi*, *Nazaraei* or *Nazorei*.)

Epiphanius tells us very little about these pre-Christian Nazarenes. The *Nasaraioi*, he wrote, accepted the authority of the patriarchs but rejected the Pentateuch, the five books of Moses containing the Torah or Laws, as not being given by God. This must be interpreted as more of a refusal to accept the law concerning Temple ritual and the cult. 'Being Jews', however, they kept Jewish practices, such as circumcision, the Sabbath and various feasts, but they rejected sacrifices and did not eat meat. They also rejected, too, the doctrine of fate (predestination?) and astrology.

It is worth mentioning that Jesus is never described as participating in acts of worship in the Temple. He did attend the synagogue, but it is not recorded that he recited psalms or took part in public prayers. The emphasis in his teachings falls on the private, unostentatious and even secret character of prayer.

Epiphanius located the pre-Christian Nazarenes in the region along the Jordan valley, and in the lands east of the upper Jordan and Sea of Galilee (the later tetrarchy of Philip). The region of Bethany, where John the Baptizer began his work, falls within this compass. These are much the same geographical locations as those associated with the later (Christian) Nazarenes. By what Epiphanius says about them, together with their location, it looks as if the *Nazaraioi* were a radical sect or cluster of groups living on the fringes – literally and metaphorically – of mainstream Israel, in the days before Jewish belief had solidified into what is now known as Judaism – a term unknown in the Bible. If indeed they existed, these Nazarenes were probably one of a number of such groups, such as the community at Qumran.

Their name suggests that they expected a Messiah from the lineage or house of David.

(3) Place

The place-derivation of 'Nazarene' has the authority of scripture. Leaving off the dialect ending, the home town of Jesus was called *Nazara* – the modern town of Nazareth is known in Arabic as *Nasariya*.

There is no mention of it in the Old Testament or in the writings of Josephus. The modern town, which lies about three miles from the site of Sepphoris, was not identified with Jesus' home town for over 300 years, Eusebius being among the first to do so (*Onomast* 138 25; 14/1). The first pilgrim to leave a memoir bypassed Nazareth in *c.* AD 330. Not until some forty years later did another pilgrim memoir mention for the first time a Christian shrine in Nazareth – a garden, cave and altar. And not until *c.* 570 is a church there mentioned. Archaeological excavations suggest that on the site of modern Nazareth there was a small agricultural settlement from about the third century BC, but there is no evidence of any public buildings in the early Roman period.

Matthew refers to the home town of Jesus as 'a city *called* Nazareth'. He uses this formula in two other places: his references to Gethsemane and Golgotha. The common denominator here is that these places had no firm name, but were known by an Aramaic name to at least some local people. It is possible, then, that the town of Jesus had another name but came to be called *Nazara* because it was colonized by a community of Nazarenes. The applied name then gave rise to the tradition that Jesus himself had lived there.

If a process along these lines does explain modern Nazareth, where else may have lain the home town of Jesus? My own suggestion is Gennesar (Aramaic 'the garden of the prince'), or Gennesaret as Galileans called it, the ancient capital of the region although in steep decline in the days of Jesus. Is there any evidence in support?

A critical passage relates to a difficult crossing of the Sea of Galilee by Jesus from east to west. In Mark's version (6:53–5) it is described as follows:

> And when they had crossed over, they came to land at Gennesaret, and moored to the shore. And when they got out of the boat, *immediately the people recognized him* [my italics], and ran about the whole neighbourhood and began to bring sick people on their pallets to any place where they heard he was.

Now it could be that these words refer to the *Plain* of Gennasaret, a fertile cultivated area about 3½ miles by 1½ miles between Magdala and the southern borders of the territory of Capernaum. But where did these people come from? They could have run a mile or two from Magdala or Capernaum, but that is unlikely.

Besides a parallel passage at 14:34, Matthew's Gospel has a more specific reference at 9:1, which tells how Jesus crossed the Sea 'and came to his *own city*' (my italics). In the *Gospel of Barnabas* (see Note 2), it is called 'the city of Nazareth'. The story of the sick people on pallets is focused in Matthew's account on one individual paralytic, a patient brought to him 'stretched out on a pallet'. Mark gives us a similar story of a paralytic, but places it earlier in his account and locates it at Capernaum. Can you see the confusion?

We know that there was a very small settlement there at the time, not far from the site of the ancient city of that name. The inland Sea of Cinnereth or Gennesaret took its name from the city, just as in the days of Jesus the new capital of Herod Antipas also led to its being known as the Sea of Tiberias. Yet Josephus tells us that the Sea was named from the adjacent *district* – the Plain of Gennesar – which suggests that the once important city of the Old Testament had long since dwindled to insignificance.

So far the archaeological investigation of the site – *Tel el-'Oreimeh* in Arabic and *Tel Kinnerat* in Hebrew – confirms this picture. Most of the mound, the citadel or acropolis of the old city, was devoid of habitation in the Hellenistic period, except for a few badly preserved houses – probably farmers who used the slope to the Lake where once the lower city lay as fields for their crops. In Roman times, it was merely a village called *Gennesar*, or *Ginnosar* in the Talmud, and that settlement can most probably be located in the vicinity of *Khirbet el-Minyeh*, a few hundred yards south of *Tell el-'Oreimeh*. Archaeologists have unearthed there a palace and mosque of the Umayyad period and the remains of a Byzantine bath house, but the site as a whole and the earlier levels of its occupation have not been excavated.

The reason for the final abandonment of the Hellenistic and Roman town or village of Gennesaret lies in the later history of the region. In the period from the fall of Jerusalem in AD 70 to about AD 150, the north-west lands abutting the Sea of Galilee – including the plain of Gennasaret – became a stronghold of orthodox Jewry. The Nazarenes – in the Talmud *ha-nozrim* – were the most despised and persecuted of the *minim*, the general Hebrew word for heretics. All Nazarenes were *minim*, but not all *minim* were Nazarenes. During this time Gennesaret became known simply as the place of the *minim*, and it is extremely probable that in this case it meant Nazarenes. For the Arab name for the site – *Khirbet* (ruins) *el-Minyeh* – reflects the name which more often than not was applied to Christians. The Hebrew name for it, significantly, is *Horvat Minnim*. The fact that Josephus does not mention Gennesaret as a town suggests that by the time of the Jewish Revolt it had, so to speak, lost its name, and was known simply as the place where the *minim* lived. Nathanael's famous comment – 'Can any good thing come out of Nazareth?' – may well reflect Jewish opinion in Galilee about Gennesaret when the Gospel of John was compiled in the early second century AD, namely that Gennesaret was a contaminated place, one that had lost its good name and was known only as the nest of the heretics.

A further point. According to the fourth Gospel, it is the inhabitants of Capernaum – not the kinsfolk of Jesus of Nazareth – who are reported as saying: 'Is not this Jesus, the son of Joseph, whose father and mother we know? How does he now say, "I have come down from heaven?"' (John 6:42). Now that comment only makes sense if the home town of Jesus was close to Capernaum, not some twenty miles away, which is where modern Nazareth lies. In this context too, it is worth adding that Nathanael – who lived in Cana less than four miles from the modern Nazareth – and Jesus did not seem to know each other before they met in the days of John the Baptizer. That is much more credible if the young Jesus lived beside the Lake and not close to Cana.

This identification of *Gennasar* (in all its variations of spelling) as the 'home town' of Jesus is potentially a major breakthrough if it holds water. It would solve several puzzles. It suggests, for example, that Jesus may have come to know – and be known by – the young fishermen of his own age or younger who lived by that part of the Lake and worked its waters.

Moreover, Luke tells us (4:23–30) that the apparent refusal of Jesus to heal the sick in Nazareth – 'what we have heard you did at Capernaum, do here also in your own country' – drove those who heard him in the city's synagogue into a sudden rage (more probably Jesus said something which was taken to be blasphemous). They resolved to kill him. Now in early Semitic societies the life of a kinsman remained sacred, whatever his misdemeanours. No one individual wanted to have his blood on their hands as an executioner, and find themselves the target in a blood feud. One solution was for all to pick up a stone and throw it, thereby sharing the blood accountability. Another solution was to cast the miscreant over a cliff, so that no individual was directly responsible for his death: 'And they rose up and put him out of the city, and led him to the brow of the hill on which their city was built, that they might throw him down headlong. But passing through the midst of them he went away.' Now the rounded hill above modern Nazareth simply would not permit such a scene. But the ground on which the city of Gennesaret stood slopes up as it nears the water's edge to a height of some 205 metres – the only place around the Lake of Galilee where we find anything like a cliff beside the shore. It is the one place where Jesus could have been cast to his death in the manner indicated in Luke 4:29.

Note 2: The Gospel of Barnabas

At first sight the apocryphal *Gospel of Barnabas* looks like an unlikely source for historical information about Jesus. As its first editors (L. and L. Ragg, *The Gospel of Barnabas*, Oxford, 1907) explain, we have only an Italian translation of it which surfaced in the early eighteenth century but is of late fifteenth- or sixteenth-century composition.

As it stands the *Gospel of Barnabas* looks like a medieval Muslim composition. But there are signs of a very early Syrian source buried within it. For example, the stormy crossing of the Sea of Galilee, when the disciples awoke Jesus, is described thus:

> They were encompassed with very great fear, by reason of the great wind that was contrary and the roaring of the sea. Jesus arose, and raising his eyes to heaven, said: 'O *Elohim Sabaoth*, have mercy upon your servants.' Then, when Jesus had said this, suddenly the wind ceased, and the sea became calm. Wherefore the boatmen feared, saying: 'And who is this, that the sea and the wind obey him?'

In the Synoptic Gospels, when Jesus was awoken he 'rebuked the wind' (Mark 4:39; Matthew 8:26; Luke 8:24); there is no mention of a prayer to God or the Hebrew/Aramaic phrase O *Elohim Sabaoth* for 'Lord God of the Hosts (of heaven)' as in Psalm 89:6–8. It was an appropriate invocation when the forces of nature were hurling themselves at the open boat. The Muslim editor was clearly mystified by the phrase, but reproduced it in a garbled form. The *Barnabas* version of the story is more Jewish in making God the author of the becalming miracle, while the

Synoptic Gospels are more Christian in seeing it as the direct result of Jesus exercising his own authority and power.

Other scholars also share my view that the first author of *Barnabas* used an early source. The French scholar Henry Corbin, in the introduction to *Evangile de Barnabe*, translated by Luigi Cirillo and Michael Fremaux (Paris: Beauchesne, 1977), speaks of *Une source primitive* or *un écrit primitif*, Jewish-Christian in origin with a Syrian, if not Palestinian, provenance. He detected in it an anti-Pauline bias. Pierre-Antoine Bernheim, in his scholarly study *James, Brother of Jesus* (1996) writes: 'It is probable that some Jewish-Christian writings have been preserved by being integrated into Islamic texts. That is *doubtless* (my italics) the case with the Jewish-Christian source used by the Muslim author of the Gospel of Barnabas, which we know only through a version in Italian dating from the sixteenth century.'

Note 3: A Bibliographical Note

The classical sources referred to, such as Plato, Arrian on Alexander, Plutarch and Herodotus, are all easily accessible in the Penguin Classics series. Xenophon's *Conversations of Socrates* in that series includes the *Memoirs of Socrates* (traditionally called the *Memorabilia*) and *The Estate-Manager*, as Xenophon's original title *Oeconomicus* is translated. A separate volume covers Xenophon's account of *The Persian Expedition*. On the Jewish side of the story, Josephus' *The Jewish War* can also be found in the same series.